Reflections of an Urban High School Principal

Bernard Gassaway

Published by XenoGass ALG,
Jamaica, New York

Copyright © 2006 by Bernard Gassaway

ISBN 13: 978-0-9769709-0-3
ISBN 10: 0-9769709-0-2

Library of Congress Control Number: 2006900376

www.bernardgassaway.com

Dedication

Hello Cooker,

You are the best mother in the world.
You've done a great job with me.
All I do now is care for others.
I am no longer the child who only
expresses himself through confusion.
Thank you for sacrificing your life,
even when I did not know how to say thank you.
I love you, Ma!
To my mother, who left this planet
on April 25, 1986

Note to the Reader

This is my story. Join me as I reflect on some of my childhood experiences growing up in the streets in Brooklyn, New York, vis-à-vis my professional experiences as a teacher, assistant principal, and principal in the New York City public school system.

I hope you walk away with the realization that we should never give up on children, especially our most challenged. By all accounts, I was a challenged youth. With support, guidance, and divine intervention, I was able to overcome tremendous odds, not unlike the children I now serve as an educator.

Acknowledgments

God is solely responsible for guiding me through the labyrinth of life. I thank her for using me as a vessel to help others.

I would like to thank my wife Traci for helping shape my voice and vision. She is my main source of strength and confidence. She has also given me the most precious gift of all, our daughter Atiya, "A gift from God."

I thank Atiya for her inspiration. She is a powerful life force.

I thank my brothers and sister for their support over the years.

I want to thank some of my teachers, the ones who believed in me, for not giving up on me.

I want to thank all of my students from PS 40Q, Boys and Girls High School, IS 59Q, Middle School 192Q, Far Rockaway High School, Beach Channel High School, and Alternative Schools and Programs.

Commitment to the Longevity and Improvement of Male Blacks (CLIMB) was an organization that worked to nurture youth in the hood. I want to give a special note of thanks to my CLIMB brothers, Beloved, Jeff, Damani, and Al. We worked together for more than twelve years serving our community.

I thank Jerome Skrine and Wayne Cox for their genuine friendship and love.

I thank the Black family court judge who, unlike the other judges, decided to take me off the streets of Brooklyn when I was quickly heading toward the cemetery.

I thank Frank N. Mickens for encouraging me to write this book.

I thank the Revson Fellowship program for helping to bring this book to life.

I thank the countless number of parents who supported my efforts over the years. I want to give special thanks to Reverend Lucille Maddox and the late Reverend Henry Maddox, PTA co-presidents at Beach Channel during my tenure as principal. God sent them to watch over the students and me.

For all who invested in me, your investment continues to yield high returns.

Table of Contents

Book III

Book IV

Book V

Preface

Here's what I know. Some of our schoolchildren live under the harshest conditions. Some are poor; some are homeless; some are parents; some are abused; some are hungry; some are incarcerated; some are confused; and some are disturbed.

Despite their station in life, when they come to school, they never expect or ask for a teacher's pity or sorrow. In fact, they may even forgive them for being incompetent. They only want respect.

For many children who are poor and of color, the educational systems across this country have never worked. Shame on all who refer to the "good ole days" when talking about education in this country. Sure, some achieved great things. A greater number never got a chance. They were deemed invisible. Like many schools today in urban communities, schools historically have been underfunded and overcrowded. Then and now, parents were told, "Hold on. Things will get better." and "We shall overcome someday." While we wait for that day, we continue to lose generation after generation.

In urban communities across this country, there is a palpable perception that white children receive a better education. I have heard too many African-American parents say, "I want my child to go to school with white kids." Although it is painful and sad to admit, I understand their logic. They believe their child has a better chance to receive a quality education with white classmates. This is an undeniable reality of racism.

Current talk among school officials focuses on closing the so-called achievement gap. This refers to the data that show white upper- and middle-class schoolchildren perform better than children of color on standardized tests. I recently attended a seminar at Columbia University for school superintendents from across the country. Closing the achievement gap was the main topic. I found this experience to be painful. They were talking about the achievement gap as if it was a math problem. One professor said we could begin to close the achievement gap if poor, minority families began behaving like middle-class whites. In his ignorant statement, he implied that poor African-Americans and other poor people could simply "wish" away their harsh reality and pretend to have the same resources and privileges as middle-class whites.

Here's what I know. Gap or no gap, children in New York City and throughout this country make it through the school system despite the odds. For the countless numbers who do not make it, no additional studies or commissions are needed to analyze the problem. We know the problem. When you are poor, you are more likely to receive a poor education. When you live in a society that believes in the "out of sight, out of mind" principle, poor people will receive a poor education. When you live in a society where more prisons are built than schools, poor people will receive a poor education. When poor people are forced to send their children to underfunded and overcrowded schools, they will continue to receive a poor education. The quality of education will not change for the vast majority of children who are poor until we attack two things with a vengeance: racism and poverty.

Book I

Introduction

On July 24, 1960, at 6:24 PM, I was born at Macon Hospital in Bibb County, Georgia. I weighed seven pounds and eight ounces. According to my birth certificate, my mother gave birth to me after forty weeks of pregnancy. She was twenty-five years old. Her race was Colored. That made me a Colored baby. All this time, I thought I was born a Negro or Black. I was brought home to 1129 Calhoun Lane, where three brothers and one sister awaited my arrival. When I was two years old, my mother moved the family to New York City.

Childhood Memories Flashback

Growing up in Bedford Stuyvesant, East New York, Crown Heights and Flatbush, all sections of Brooklyn, New York, with a mother, grandmother, three brothers and three sisters helped to shape my profound passion for the welfare of children growing up in similar circumstances. I watched my mother raise us on little to nothing. We lived from month to month, check to check. I remember my Pavlovian reaction as the first and the sixteenth of each month approached. That's when the mailman delivered the welfare checks.

I remember my mother getting a face-to-face letter from my school to take to the welfare office. The letter was referred to as "face-to-face" because she had to personally appear before the social services people to present the letter. I know now that she had to prove her children were attending school. During these visits, she faced degradation from social workers, security guards, and a host of social service employees, only to keep the handouts coming to support her family.

I remember playing some serious basketball on the building's fire escapes. Because the ball would cause the fire escape to rattle, some people would periodically complain. Most wouldn't, probably out of fear. I also remember playing a full-court game of basketball on metal garbage cans. We were serious. We assumed the roles of pros like Walt Clyde Frazier and Earl "The Pearl" Monroe. We were Oscar Robinson or Wilt Chamberlain when we shot foul shots. They both had unusual releases. We played basketball all year long in the streets or in the park. We played our most exciting games at night without gloves in the snow.

I remember playing in the Johnny Pump (Some of you may know it as a fire hydrant). We'd use a can with both ends opened to spray water at each other and at cars. Periodically the firemen or police would turn the water off. We'd then turn it back on after they left.

I remember when the fellas would begin our mornings pitching pennies, which would grow to dimes and then quarters. At some point someone would pull out dice or we'd chip in to buy three dice. Old-timers preferred playing craps which required two dice. Younger folk played Ci-Lo which required three dice.

I remember when I tried boxing in a ring for the first time. I got beat down, and that was the end of my boxing aspirations. The gloves were so heavy! I stuck to street fighting. There was only one rule. The fight was over when one person told the other, "You got it." That would end the fight. There was an unwritten code. Once the person submitted, the fight was over. Period!

I remember velvet posters. Some glowed in the dark. We used black light bulbs.

I remember eating powdered eggs. We would open the container, pour the powder into a pan, and mix water. I have no idea who thought of this food. It was readily available from welfare. I also remember the infamous welfare cheese. The cheese would not melt. It was nearly impossible to make a grilled cheese sandwich, but we did.

I remember being very creative when we didn't have any food in the refrigerator. My favorite meal substitute was a sugar sandwich. I only needed two pieces of bread and some sugar.

I remember lying about being on welfare. At least ninety percent of my friends were on welfare. During our childhood, we all denied it.

I remember lying about having a father. I would say he worked at night. That's why my friends never met him. They never challenged me. In all likelihood, they were also lying about their fathers' whereabouts.

I remember seeing junkies nodding on the street. They would nod slowly to the ground. I never saw a junkie fall during a nod. It was the ultimate balancing act.

I remember when we hung out and talked about sex. Older guys bragged about how long they would have sex. They'd go for hours at a time. Not! They also discussed the size of their anatomy. With a smile, they'd say how they would hurt a girl during sex. So, we grew up thinking we needed to have rough sex and last for hours at a time to satisfy a woman.

I remember my friends put me up to ask an older girl to be my girlfriend. I was ten. She was twelve. I nervously whispered, "Will you go with me?" She yelled, "No!" I felt so embarrassed. I never asked that question of anyone else.

I remember we knew the winos on the street. They had names, and people would bring plates of food to them. Our local winos were Scotty and Slim. Now, people simply refer to winos as home-less people.

I remember we were respectful around adults, especially the elderly.

I remember when you could buy sneakers (rejects) for $1.99. The tease would go like this, Rejects, they cost a $1.99. Rejects, they make your feet feel fine.

I remember canvas PRO-Keds and Converse sneakers (about ten dollars).

I remember having the same artificial Christmas tree forever. It was not even green. It was silver. I don't think we ever had a real tree in our house.

I remember when you could buy ten cookies for a dime. For a quarter, you could get a complete sugar meal. This consisted of candy, cookies, chips and a juice (It was a high-octane meal that tasted like sweetened gasoline).

I remember people would drink from the same soda or beer bottle. Someone would even be proud to drink the foamy suds at the end of the bottle. Damn! That's nasty!

I remember watching my mother read the Bible. She would also copy verses into a little book she had. I imagine this was how she practiced writing and reading.

I remember hearing my mother sing, "What a Friend We Have in Jesus."

I remember listening to my mother speak of Jesus and God as if she knew them personally. "Lord, what am I gonna to do with these children? I'm gonna give them up to you."

I remember hearing mice chewing on the inner wall plaster. One day I put on my sneakers and noticed one foot felt tighter than usual. I went about my day. At some point mid-day, I took off the sneaker that was hurting my foot. I hit the sneaker on the floor to dislodge whatever was in it. A mouse dropped out. At first, it appeared to be dead. After I screamed, it came out of its coma and ran.

I remember going to church as a child. We "people watched." I could see the preacher but his words had little to no meaning to me. I enjoyed the singing and watching the usherettes walking in unison as they sang "It's a Highway to Heaven." Whenever I think of church I think of hard shoes and sore feet. My shoes always hurt. My mother would say, "Boy, you will break them in." I grew up thinking that you should always break your shoes in. Years later, one day my wife took me to buy a pair of Ballys made of soft leather. I said, Damn! I cannot believe this is how shoes are supposed to feel." I have never worn a hard pair of shoes again. I will go shoe-less before I torture my feet with that hard imitation leather.

I remember the infamous unwanted houseguests, roaches. Damn! They were everywhere. I thought all families had roaches. They would come out and crawl when company came over. Embarrassing! They would come out in full force in darkness. I would stomp on the floor before I entered the kitchen at night. I would do this to alert the roaches of my presence before turning on the light. Once I turned on the light, the roaches made a mad dash for the cabinets. I eventually got tired of trying to kill them. There were so many. Raid was like cologne to them.

I remember our role models being pimps and convicts. We often talked in glowing terms about convicts who had reputations for being hard-core criminals and good fighters.

I remember when we looked forward to eating school lunches. Before schools began to serve breakfast, we would leave from home early to get free breakfast at a local church on New York Avenue.

I remember packing groceries at the local supermarket. This was a nice honest hustle. We would offer to carry bags for customers to their cars. More likely we would take them to their homes. Not many people in the hood had cars. If they did, they did not usually shop in our neighborhood. Interestingly, adults have co-opted this particular hustle today. It's a sign of the times.

I remember thinking I would never die. That God would make an exception for me. I heard of a biblical character that did not die. He rode his chariot straight to heaven.

I remember my mother would take in any relatives who migrated from the south. She had a giving heart.

I remember my mother always sacrificed for us. She deprived herself. She probably never had her own bedroom. She never saw a play or dined at a fine restaurant. Damn!

I remember my mother saying, "Boy, God don't like ugly."

Oh yeah! I remember when Grandmothers were over sixty years old. They used to make biscuits from scratch.

Elementary School Teacher

On October 14, 1986, after briefly serving as a substitute teacher at several schools, I began my full-time teaching career at PS 40 in South Jamaica, Queens. I was given a class that had two teachers in the one month since school opened. The students told me they would run me out, as they had succeeded with the others. Next!

I had about thirty students. Nearly all were functioning years below their grade level.

That year, I averaged about four hours of sleep each night. I, along with Traci, my wife, would spend many hours planning lessons. I was determined to teach my students, whether they were willing to learn or not. On countless occasions, because of behavioral disruptions, I was unable to teach the lessons I had prepared. Anytime something went awry in a particular lesson, I asked myself, "What did I do wrong?" You see, I was new at this. It took hours—sometimes days—to develop lesson motivations. Each motivation was designed to hold the students' interests for the forty-minute period.

Even though I received a tremendous amount of support from my principal, assistant principal and fellow teachers, I could not seem to convince my students that I was trying to teach them something important. Like Siddhartha, I searched all over trying to find "it." What would "it" take? Yelling did not work. Phones calls, letters, and home visits did not work either. I do not remember the exact moment, but "it" came to me. I realized "it" was always in front of me. I needed to drop the script. Until that point, I was acting, acting like a teacher. I focused so much on my lessons that I forgot about my students. Once I dropped the script, I became real to them. I realized it was okay to let them see Bernard.

My ability to teach also depended on my ability to communicate with my students. When I changed my approach and philosophy, I began getting through to them. I was no longer the teacher in front of the students. I became the teacher among the students. We were in it together. We began having fun. I took them on trips. These students were not accustomed to trips. Their behavior caused teachers to leave individual students at school or not take the class. Even when they did not believe in themselves, I believed in them. I listened to everything they said, even unspoken words. This proved to be the most significant ingredient in our relationship.

Later, I realized I saw in my students what my teachers might have seen in me. On the surface, I was this stern, calloused child. Behind the façade, I wanted to be recognized and valued. I valued each student as an individual. No magic. It works.

Elementary School Flashback

I recently acquired a copy of my elementary school records. Surprisingly, the records did not match my memory of my academic ability. In fact, schoolwork did not seem particularly challenging to me. I rarely needed to do homework because I would do it during "free time" in class. Anyhow, this is how my teachers described me:

First Grade	Very aggressive at times. Sometimes refuses to answer you or do any work. He has no close friends in class. Needs attention.
Second Grade	Bernard does no work and fights a great deal with other children.
Second Grade	Bernard has shown much improvement.
Third Grade	Bernard shows both extremes—complete self-control or complete uncontrolled attitude.
Fourth Grade	Bernard has made a lot of progress academi-

	cally and socially. He is very intelligent and lovable.
Fifth Grade	Bernard requires personal attention at times. He is a very fast worker, but he becomes restless at times. He seems to control his aggressiveness at this point. Extremely reliable and tries to cooperate.

I found each description focued on my behavior. Throughout elementary school, I distinctly remember finishing my work before my classmates. The teachers would direct me to work independently from the SRA kit. The kit had reading comprehension assignments with answer keys so I could check my answers. The assignments ranged from easy to difficult. I spent a lot of time with the SRA kit. It became very boring. That's when trouble found me.

I am sure I held the record for most suspensions in elementary school. It seems as if I was suspended every other week. As per school policy, I stayed home during my periods of suspension. I was probably suspended more for defiance of authority than fighting. Two suspensions stick out in my mind. I was suspended for five days. I returned to school on Monday. I was then suspended on Tuesday for another week. My mother tried disciplining me the only way she knew. Literally, she tried beating the hell out me.

The school mandated that my mother make weekly visits to the school to see my teachers and guidance counselor. The school eventually required I see a child psychiatrist at Brooklyn Jewish Hospital. I only recall playing board games during my visits. This continued for about a year before the sessions ended. I am not sure why they ended.

Looking back on my elementary school experience, I believe the school officials lowered the threshold for what they would accept from me. I will never doubt that some of their actions were justified.

However, there were those times when it seemed as if suspension was their answer for the smallest infractions, especially in my case.*

*Interestingly, even today in 2005, school officials continue to believe that suspension is the optimal remedy when dealing with so-called disruptive children. I was guilty of this practice when I was a principal.

Middle School Teacher/ Assistant Principal

I was fortunate to work with my students at PS 40. They prepared me for my eventual future as a teacher and administrator. After PS 40, I moved on to teach high school and middle school students. Teaching on the middle school level was difficult. I recall one specific incident when I was confronted by a student who was disrupting the class. I told him to go to the dean's office. He stood up and, within inches, got right in my face. He clenched his fists. I thought, "If he hits me, I'm going to knock the hell out of him." My heart began to race. I knew I would lose my job if I hit him, even in self-defense. We stared at each other for about a minute, which seemed like an hour. The entire gym class of about fifty students looked on in complete silence. For some reason, he backed down. I do not know why. He left the class on his own accord.

As I reflect on this incident, I believe this young man wanted attention from me. He desired a male relationship but did not know how to establish it. He responded in the only way he knew how. After all, he was competing for my attention with at least fifty other students. I could have easily been his first African-American male teacher. Like me, he probably did not have an adult male authority figure in his life. As I think back to my childhood, I resented any man, especially Black men, trying to tell me what to do. So, when this student confronted me, ironically, I felt a kinship with him. I was exactly like this student when I was his age. He was confused by his history and circumstances.

After the standoff in the gym, I did not have any problems with this student.

After approximately eight years in the classroom, I decided I needed to earn my second master's degree in school supervision and administration. I wanted to become an assistant principal. I felt I could make a greater impact on a larger number of students.

I got my first assistant principal assignment at the Linden Middle School 192 in Queens, New York. I began this assignment in February 1994. It almost ended as quickly as it began. I supervised the sixth grade. I will never forget a particular incident. One after-noon after lunch, I was sitting in my office when I heard the familiar sound of people running through the fourth-floor corridor. I ran to the door and noticed two young people who stood around six foot tall. They did not appear to be students. Without thinking, I grabbed one of the boys. The other boy stopped at the exit door and yelled, "Shoot him! Shoot that nigga!"

What do you think I did? I let him go. They ran down the stairs and probably left the building. I said to myself, "Damn! I did not take this job to die." I left this assignment in June.

Middle School Flashback

In September 1971, I began junior high school at 61K, Lefferts Junior High School, in Brooklyn. For some reason, I was placed in the top sixth-grade class, 6–1.* I am not sure why. I believed I was smart and not really challenged in elementary school. I also knew I got in a lot of trouble. So this class assignment had me confused.

I was not happy. I could not relate to the teachers and the students. All of my friends from around the way were in a special class called 6-109. It was a smaller class for what may have been described as disruptive students. I wanted to be placed in that class. So I began my journey of disruption. My strategy worked. In one year, I went from 6–1 to 6–7 to 6–10 to 6–109. Students in 6–1 were

*Students were grouped by ability. The number following the grade indicated your academic standing. The lowest number represented the higher functioning class. I believe this practice, in some form, continues in many schools.

not my cup of tea. I was so happy to make it to 6–109. I felt more at home in this smaller setting. Moreover, I could definitely relate more to my peers and the teacher, Mr. Lebowitz.

When I was in the seventh grade, a white male teacher slapped the hell out of me. I left school and went home to tell my mother. As a good parent would do, she immediately returned to school with me to confront the teacher. When the assistant principal explained the circumstances behind the teacher's actions, my mother then slapped me. I failed to tell her that I pulled the teacher's fractured thumb. Because of the way it was bandaged, it was obviously fractured. I do not remember why I pulled his thumb. I think he tried to block me from leaving the classroom.

I was absent twenty-two days in the seventh grade. The following year, I was absent fifty-four days. I attended two schools in the eighth grade because we had to move due to a fire in our building. Even though we speculated that some drunk fell asleep while smoking, the actual cause of the fire was never officially determined. We even suspected the landlord set the fire to collect insurance money.

"Welfare" relocated the entire family to a homeless shelter, the Granada Hotel in downtown Brooklyn. I have few memories of life in the shelter. I do remember eating spiced ham sandwiches and the occasional Chinese food treat. To this day, I will not eat spiced ham because of the memories it conjures up for me. The shelter did not allow families to cook. They probably did not trust the families with fire. Many of us were there because we had been burned out of our apartments.

After this brief stay in a welfare hotel, we moved to 923 Dumont Avenue in the East New York section of Brooklyn. I briefly attended Junior High School 64K. By now, I was spending the majority of my time running the streets. Obviously, my grades reflected my attendance. Interestingly, I managed to never be held back for any grade. Social promotion was in full effect.*

After roughly eight months living in East New York, we moved to 800 Nostrand Avenue in the Crown Heights section of Brooklyn. I was transferred back to Lefferts Junior High School. Now in the ninth grade, I was completely off the hook. Routinely, I was suspended for reasons including defiance of authority, disrespect, fights, and robbery. I was probably out of school more days than in. The administration was looking for a reason to get rid of me. Finally, sometime during the winter of 1974, I set a bulletin board on fire. A teacher identified me as I ran out of the building. The next thing I know, I was expelled and transferred to what was called a "600 School," Sterling High School.

---

*Social promotion occurs when a student is advanced to the next grade because of his age instead of his academic performance.

High School Assistant Principal

My most treasured memory of 1994 was the birth of my daughter Atiya. She was born on August 26, 1994. As fate would have it, three days later, I began my new assignment as assistant principal of guidance at Far Rockaway High School. What happened next almost changed the course of history for my family and me. Five days after her birth, Atiya had to be hospitalized.

My wife and I decided she would breastfeed Atiya. We thought it would be simple, but we didn't know Traci was dehydrated. She lost scores of fluids during her forty-eight hour labor. As a result, Atiya was not getting milk from Traci's breasts. We were completely unaware. Traci and I noticed Atiya was not urinating as often as we thought she should. We took her to our pediatrician. Of course, she urinated on the doctor during this visit. We were relieved, so we took her home. A day passed, she again did not urinate. We called the doctor and said Atiya was not active and listless. The doctor told us to immediately take her to the emergency room. We got in the car. I frantically drove through streetlights, hoping for the police to stop us. I foolishly thought they would give us an emergency escort. We were trying to make it to Queens Booth Memorial Hospital, and we made it. The receptionist told us to have a seat.

I screamed, "I need help now! My baby is not breathing!"

"Calm down."

Needless to say, I did not sit, and I did not calm down. We were immediately assisted. Traci and I could barely see beyond our tears and fears. Our baby lying listless with medical personnel trying to diagnose her ailment was almost too much to bear. They decided Atiya needed a spinal tap. After they explained what it entailed, sticking a needle in the base of her spine and drawing fluids, I went into that "take me Lord" stage. I am sure parents can relate to that. She was too young and innocent. Moments before they were to begin the procedure, Atiya's pediatrician, Dr. Ruby Malva, enters. She immediately took charge. The emergency room doctors and staff automatically gave her deference. She dismissed the recommendation for a spinal tap. Honestly, I am unclear about what happened next. It was determined that Atiya would be hospitalized for testing. She suspected that Atiya was dehydrated, but she wanted to see if she had liver damage. Atiya remained in the hospital for fourteen days. My wife and I would not leave her alone. We took turns. I took the night shift; she took the day shift.

Keep in mind, I would sleep in her room and go home in the morning. I'd take a shower and go to work. During my first days at the job, I was not focused. I met with the principal, Minnie Richardson, and offered to resign. At that time and under those circumstances, I realized I was unable to do the job that needed to be done. She told me to hang in there. She provided me with flexibility to handle my personal situation. I am grateful for her act of compassion during the most difficult days of my life. After fourteen days, Traci and I brought our healthy baby girl, Atiya, "A gift from God," home.

I worked at Far Rockaway High School until I left to become principal of Beach Channel High School in April 1997.

High School Flashback

Sterling High School was an all-boys school with grades nine through twelve. I felt comfortable when I arrived there in February 1975. I knew a few students from my neighborhood; they had my back. It was a neighborhood thing. By the time I attended Sterling, I was fully engaged in street life. I had little or no interest in school. I hustled, got high, and hung hard in the streets, twenty-four seven. My initial stay at Sterling was short-lived, probably one month. I was cutting class when I ran across the dean of students. After a brief verbal confrontation, I called him a "fucking faggot." He then threw a bag of tokens at me. (At the end of the day, all students were given two tokens: one to get home and one to return the next day. They did not trust us with bus or train passes. They figured, if we were given passes, we would probably use them to cut school and ride the trains. They were absolutely correct.) Anyway, this chance encounter with the dean provided justification to stop going to school altogether. At the time, this was my rationale.

After yet another arrest, I had a court date. It would be the first time I stood before a Black judge. Over the years, I had been before all-white male judges and even a blind judge. My visits were routine. I would be released to my mother's custody. I did not have any idea this chance encounter with a "brother" would change the course of my life. When he told my mother that I would not be going home with her, I began crying like a baby. Fortunately, my homeboys did not see me. They would have called me a punk.

At the height of my juvenile delinquency, I was taken off the streets of New York City and sent to Annsville Youth Camp, in Taberg, New York, near Utica. The New York State Division for Youth ran this facility. I was fortunate to be sent to Annsville. The judge had actually sentenced me to Warwick State Facility for Boys for eighteen months. Warwick was a facility for hard-core delinquents.

I am one hundred percent convinced that my journey to Annsville in 1975 saved my life. I was quickly approaching the "I don't give a fuck" stage. This is the most dangerous stage for any person, especially a juvenile. Nothing matters. You don't even care if you live or die. So, the judge essentially gave me a second chance at life when he took me off the streets of Brooklyn.

Once at Annsville, they provided counseling, adult relationships, education, and a relatively tranquil environment. If I had to specifically describe what helped turn my life around, it would be the significant relationships that were established with adults. The counselors, teachers, and cooks seemed to genuinely care about the residents. When I began teaching, this would influence my relationship with children.

On July 17, 1976, I was released from Annsville. I served eight of the eighteen months. Basically, I did not cause any trouble. There were the occasional runaway incidents. I do not recall getting into fights besides the ritual "jailhouse boxing." During this time, I attended classes and began taking my studies seriously. I knew I was intelligent. I was just bored to hell in public school.

In September 1976, I returned to Sterling High School. I returned a focused student, and everyone noticed the change. However, I was not completely rehabilitated. I was later arrested for the last time for trespassing. The police confiscated the property in our makeshift clubhouse. They did not have any clue that it was stolen property from a burglary. This arrest was different from all previous encounters with police. Because I was sixteen years old, I was considered an adult. I was fingerprinted, photographed, and strip-searched. That was the last straw for me. After spending one night in a cold cell, my legal aid attorney and the prosecutor made a deal. He said, "You can go to trial or plead guilty to trespassing and go home today." I did not have a choice. My mother could not pay bail. I said, "I want to go home!"

I did not feel the same as I did before going to Annsville. My time away from my homeboys helped extinguish my burning desire to be in the streets. I began thinking about my future.

By this time, I had determined two things. I needed to get serious about school, and I needed to change my friends. I hooked up with two guys from Sterling named Jerome and Gerry. Our favorite pastime was playing basketball. I joined the school's basketball team. My social studies teacher helped get me a job at a local Key Food supermarket.

One particular event at Sterling would have a lasting impression on me. My English teacher recommended me for the Student of the Year award. Academically, I had made a significant amount of progress. I won academic contests. The staff recognized me as one of the students who took his studies seriously. Surprisingly, I won the award. However, I did not know that the award was for students who were classified as emotionally handicapped. This was an affectionate classification primarily applied to children of color that school officials could not figure out. I knew something was strange about the award when I attended the ceremony to receive it. My mother and I arrived early. We were the first to sit at our table. As the other student awardees entered in wheelchairs and wearing helmets, we began thinking we were in the wrong place. Apparently, they were physically and mentally challenged. I was bugging out. It all hit me. When my teacher first announced the award, I did ask myself, "Damn. How did I deserve to be Student of the Year of all the high school students in the city?"

The answer became clear when I was given my certificate. The certificate read:

New City Chapter, New York State Association of Teachers of the Handicapped, Inc., proudly presents this award to Bernard Gassaway, 1978 Outstanding Pupil of the Year, signed by Chairperson for the Pupil of the Year Committee Susan Strian May and President of the New York State Chapter Joel M. Klein. *

When my mother and I left the award program, we laughed so hard. I never recall seeing my mother have such a good, healthy laugh. She said, "You see what they think about when you act a fool." I do not believe she ever fully understood why I behaved one way at home and another way at school.

When I returned to school, I felt differently. I felt stigmatized. I felt "special ed." My feelings were validated when one of the teachers who congratulated me said, "Congratulations. Now you are normal again." Imagine hearing that from your teacher. I responded to this thunderous insult with complete silence. This

---

*This is not the current New York City school's chancellor. His name is Joel I. Klein.

experience and others would have a profound impact on me as an educator. Ironically, some twenty years later, now as principal, students in our so-called special education department would be nominated for a similar award.

When I won this award, the label of emotionally handicapped became relevant to me. I do not recall ever receiving an evaluation to receive this classification. They, the school officials, did whatever they wanted. I do not doubt that my behavior gave them cause for concern. However, an emotionally handicapped classification was arbitrarily assigned to me. The same was true for many of my contemporaries.

The following is a letter from my English teacher who recommended me for the award:

> *December 19, 1977*
> *Dear Bernard,*
> *It has been my pleasure to watch your soaring academic progress! You have used your time to pursue academic excellence, and I want you to continue to realize the importance of time. As your teacher, I am proud of you!*
> *This small present is a token of my admiration for your success. My wish is for you to continue the fine job you have begun!*
> *All the best,*
> *Shaharagad J. Kleindienst*

Welcome to Beach Channel High School

I was assigned as the first African-American principal of Beach Channel High School on April 28, 1997.

Beach Channel High School was not unlike many urban high schools. We served grades nine through twelve. Our enrollment ranged from 1,800 to 2,200. We had a diverse student body, including:

- 16.5% White
- 53.7% Black
- 26.5% Hispanic
- 3.3% Other

Even though we had our share of problems, we had many success stories. I have found that many children succeed despite the quality of the education they receive. They succeed despite the challenges of their community and home conditions. They are resilient.

By any objective analysis, Beach Channel was a school on the verge of disaster when I arrived. During a tour of the building, I noticed the halls never cleared of students. Some were standing in line, waiting to use one of the many vending machines or purchase a bagel from the student-run bagel shop. Others were simply not moving, even after staff told them to move. As much student traffic as I observed inside the school, an equal amount of traffic was taking place outside the school. It was almost overwhelming to witness.

College Flashback

I never really thought about attending college until Jerome graduated from Sterling and began college. You see, none of my former friends ever talked about college. Instead, we talked of being able to survive in prison. We talked about what we believed was the glamorous life of being a pimp. So, when Jerome went to college and came back to talk about his experiences, he motivated me. He encouraged me to attend his school. I, along with my physical education teacher and basketball coach, Mr. Horace Jones, began the college application process. To my surprise, I was accepted to three colleges: Saint Augustine in North Carolina, Elizabeth City in North Carolina, and LeMoyne College in Syracuse, New York. I decided to attend LeMoyne. Ralph Gaston, my brother-in-law, had attended LeMoyne in the early 1970s. He is the one who brought my case to the director of the Higher Education Opportunity Program (HEOP), Carl Thomas. HEOP was a program that was designed to enable poor, academically challenged students to attend college, provided they demonstrated potential for success while in high school. I was initially placed on a waiting list. Fortunately, someone withdrew their application at the last minute and made the way for me.

LeMoyne presented some challenges for me. One particular experience stands above the rest. I remember it as if it was yesterday. I was probably the only Black student in my English 101 class. I knew the day would come. I anticipated it with dread. The professor would eventually call on me to read aloud in front of the entire class, as was his practice during round-robin reading of a novel. Each time I got out of class without hearing my name called, I'd breathe a sigh of relief. Today was my day.

"Bernard, please read the next paragraph."

I nearly stopped breathing because I was so nervous. If this had happened when I was in junior high school, I would have acted like a fool to distract the class. Because this was college, I began reading. After reading about four sentences, I misread the word "diaphragm" for "diagram." As if on cue, the entire class began laughing. To add insult to injury, the professor also began laughing. He laughed so hard that tears were in his eyes. Or were they tears in my eyes? I felt the need to punch somebody … anybody. Instead, I did nothing. The laughter stopped after what seemed like an eternity. I refused to read any further. I do not remember the professor calling me to read for the rest of the semester. That was fine by me. I did continue to feel crazed by the looming anticipation though.

I decided to turn this embarrassing moment into an opportunity to rid myself of my true handicap, an inferior education. I knew my formal educational experience was inferior to that of my classmates. Somehow, I could tell the difference between having an inferior education and being an inferior being. The only way I could reverse my educational inferiority was to work extremely hard. I did that. I began studying on Friday and Saturday nights. The school library was usually empty because these were party nights. I received a C in this English class. As a senior, I took this professor for a second course. I needed to prove something to him and to myself. I could earn an A. Yes, I did earn an A. The humiliated freshman was now the triumphant senior. I graduated in four years and earned my bachelor of arts degree in English. I immediately enrolled in the State University of Albany, where I earned my first master's degree in public administration.

A Day I Will Never Forget

We were finishing a meeting when my secretary said I had an emergency call from one of the vice presidents from Peninsula Hospital. He wanted me to locate two students and have them brought to the hospital immediately. The students were cousins. Reportedly, both of their mothers were seriously injured in a car accident and were near death. I was told not to mention the circumstances to the students. Before they arrived at my office, I received a second call informing me that one of the parents had died. I did not know whose parent had died. When the students came to my office, it was extremely difficult to look at them and know that one of them was about to receive the worst news they could imagine. As the two students walked into my office, tears began flowing down the face of the female.*

*I was later informed that her mother was the one who had passed.

Her male cousin began screaming, "What happened?"

I said, "Your mothers were in a car accident. They want you at the hospital."

Along with two guidance counselors, I waited outside of the school for what seemed like an eternity for a taxicab to arrive. I nearly broke department of education policy to drive the students in my personal vehicle. The taxicab did come, and I sent the two counselors to accompany them to the hospital. I began running toward the school. I made it to my office door. I fumbled to get my keys in the door. I did not want anyone to see me cry. I did not make it. Emotions overcame me. I cried uncontrollably, the kind where snot runs down your nose. I cried hard. I believe I was actually grieving my own mother's death.

Mother's Love Flashback

Sometime during the summer of 1985, news of my mother's breast cancer came without warning. None of us ever expected our mother to get sick. It was her job to take care of her seven children and her mother (some of us selfishly thought). When I heard the news, I was in shock, albeit hopeful she would overcome this challenge as she had overcome so many others. Even after the doctors determined she would lose both of her breasts, the notion of death still did not hit me. After what seemed like a short hospital stay, she was brought home, practically spiritless. She seemed to carry her ailing body just enough to give us, her seven children, a little hope. I watched my mother deteriorate right before my eyes. Miraculously, after receiving news from her doctors that the operation was "successful,"she seemed to regain strength. She began drinking nasty-tasting juices. She believed these health juices would provide her body with energy. This gave her a sense of hope.

Before the discovery of her illness, she had finally been able to establish what appeared to be a meaningful relationship with a man named Freddy. This was difficult for her to do over the years. You see, we, her children, required too much of her attention. Freddy was aware of one rule: you ever hit my mother, and we will kill you. When my mother returned home from surgery, Freddy chose not to handle it. He criticized her for having her breast removed. He left her when she needed manly affection most. From that moment on, she probably never acknowledged her womanhood.

One day, several months following her operation and major chemotherapy sessions, she was asked to make an unscheduled visit to the doctor. They told her to bring someone—someone strong—with her. Of all her children, she chose me. I often wondered, "Why me?"

I drove her to Sloan-Kettering on a sunny, wintry day. We arrived at the hospital and remained in the waiting room. I saw a baby in the stroller waiting to see the doctor.

I said to myself, "Damn. This poor child has never even experienced life and has cancer." The lead doctor called us in. We sat in a small office. She asked my mother how she was feeling.

My mother nervously said, "Fine."

"Ms. Gassaway, the cancer has spread. It is in your spine and liver. We cannot do anymore."

My mother began crying. I fought, unsuccessfully, to restrain my tears. I was supposed to be there for support. We left the hospital as fast as we entered. In the car going home, we both said little or nothing at all.

When we arrived home to the projects, I thought, "This is the essence of being poor. There is no justifiable reason for her to live under such horrific conditions. Pissy, broken elevators ... roaches ... rats ... crime ... an abundance of human misery. If she has to die, let her die with dignity."

I wanted so much to enable my mother to see the better parts of life. She lived all of her adult life for her children and others. She did not want much. She wanted her children to be fed and get a good education.

This cancer thing just messed everything up. She was supposed to live forever. Even on her deathbed, she was concerned about her children and her mother. She would hold back expressions of pain, just to spare her children sorrow. We told her that we would be all right. I even yelled at her to stop worrying herself so much. None of us knew how to handle my mother's illness. Roughly two months after the doctor so bluntly told us of her terminal cancer, she was taken to the hospital for the last time. We visited her daily to watch her seething body wince as frequent doses of morphine were given to her. We took turns yelling at the nurses to give her more morphine. As her eyes filled with crust, we knew the end was near. On April 25, 1986, I got that call. My supervisor broke the news to me. I was pissed my family member told her instead of talking directly with me. When I arrived at the hospital, my brother Randy was walking down the street.

He said, "She's gone."

I did not react. I did not cry.

Twenty Years Later— Letter to My Mother

2002

Hello Ma,

It has been twenty years since you died. There are times when it only seems like yesterday. I have so much I want to say to you. First, let me tell you about Atiya. She is your granddaughter. What a joy. She would have made you so happy. You and Norma would probably be fighting over her.

Traci and I are still together. I know you probably had your doubts about me. She has stuck with me even when she had reasons to leave. I sometimes feel I have not fulfilled the promises of our unspoken prenuptial agreement. By the way, Traci truly loves you. Yeah, Atiya loves you, too. She even talks about conversations she has with you. That's between you and her.

Ma, would you believe I became a teacher? I know this brings you both joy and surprise. You must be laughing because of all the hell I caused my teachers. I also decided to become a school principal.

I love you. I love you everyday. I hope to make up for all the days I failed to say "I love you." Do you remember the first time I said it to you? I think I was in college. I loved you all of my life. I just did not know how to tell you. I know my behavior said other things, especially, "I don't care!"

I wish you had a chance to visit Las Vegas. Your doctors did not think it was a good idea for you to travel. I wanted to give you so many things. I definitely wanted to buy you a house. You deserved a home of your own. I always wanted to ask you how you managed to take care of your seven children, your mother, and every cousin who visited from the South. You even welcomed strangers into our house and treated them like family. Why? I know it was godly.

Speaking of God, I long to hear you sing your religious songs. "What a friend we have in Jesus ..." I used to notice you writing verses from the Bible. Was that your way of practicing your writing? I was convinced you loved God. At the time, I was not convinced that God loved you. Now I know he did. When I look at Atiya, I realize that, without you, there would be no her.

Ma, I have so many of your habits. I get up early every morning. I seem to worry about everything. I try to take care of everybody, but it's definitely not to the same degree as you did.

Ma, I apologize for all of the nights I stayed out without you knowing my whereabouts. I now know that, every time you heard a siren, you thought they were going after me. Every time you heard a gunshot or smash of a bottle, I know you thought it was meant for me. I wish I could make up for all of the hours you spent at the window waiting for me to come home in the early morning hours. I sincerely apologize for the pounds of aggravation I caused you. I do not know what possessed me to act in such ways. Whether it was in school or the judicial system, I did not realize the embarrassment I caused you, visit after visit. God, what those people must have thought of you. I feel sorry for parents when they visit me regarding their misbehaving children. I think of you each time.

What I would give to see you walking down the street pushing your shopping cart full of welfare food: powdered eggs, cheese, and butter. I was embarrassed when you asked me to help you carry the food to the house. What I would not give to see you now.

Ma, your cooking is legendary. We still talk about your fried chicken and potato salad. I think you have inspired Traci and Denise. They would proudly submit that they can only come close.

Do you remember when Randy, Eleanor, and I were arguing over who should get to lick the cake bowl? You became so frustrated that you threw the cake out of the window. That shocked the hell out of us. I was so tempted to go outside, kiss the cake up to God, and eat it anyway. We sit around now and laugh at our foolishness. I find myself saying things you said to us to Atiya. "Atiya, I will throw that ice cream away if you are not grateful!"

Ma, it's wild that I waited until you died to ask a thousand questions about your life. I want to know so much about you. Actually, I want the world to know about your generosity and tenacity.

I hope you are not upset that I am trying to get informa-

tion on the white man who raped you when you were seven-teen. I just found out that you were pregnant with Cass when he did that to you. I love you so much.

Thank you for not parading men in and out of my life and having me call someone "Daddy." All I know about my biological father is that you loved him. That is good enough for me. If you loved him, I could not hate anything you loved. For years, I told myself it did not matter if I knew my father. After forty-two years of life, I have finally come to believe that my father in my life could have made a difference. I think about this when I look at my relationship with Atiya. I could not imagine life without being in her life.

Ma, I often tell the story how I did not go to the graduation ceremony in Albany. In hindsight, I should have attended for you. I missed the opportunity to see you cry tears of joy. I remember your crying face at LeMoyne's graduation. You were so proud. You must have recounted all the times you came to the precinct to pick me up and all the nights I defiantly did not come home, just because I wanted to hang with the fellas a little longer. What I would not do to take back all of that foolishness.

You give me so much strength. In your memory, I have devoted my life to serving others, particularly our children. I want to spare many mothers the pain and suffering you so aptly endured.

You never stopped loving us, even when our actions seemed to reject your love.

Ma, when I see parents struggling with their children, especially their boys, I often think of you. I actually feel pain because I know you went through the same struggles with me. I guess that's, in part, why I work so hard to help develop young boys today.

Book II

From Chaos to Community

On April 25, 1997, a rainy Friday morning, I arrived at Beach Channel High School to meet the staff and talk to the outgoing principal. I was introduced to the staff in the main lobby. One by one, they came. Many shook my hand and introduced themselves.

I thought, "There is no way I could remember the names of all these people."

This continued for about twenty minutes. Then my predecessor thought it would be a good idea to introduce me to the students who were waiting in the auditorium for the first period bell to sound. She was given a microphone that malfunctioned as she spoke.

I said to myself, "They probably cannot understand what she is saying because of the short in the cord."

When she made it through her comments, I was introduced and given a bullhorn. I did not miss the likely comparison to Joe Clark, the former celebrated principal of Eastside High School in New Jersey. My remarks were brief. I was self-conscious about speaking through that damn bullhorn.

After the meet and greet, the principal took me on a tour of the building.

I was looking forward to Monday, my first official day as principal. I asked the superintendent if I could skip the citywide principals' retreat that was scheduled for that week. He granted my request.

On either my second or third day on the job, all hell broke loose. There were seven fights in one day. I was walking through the halls when a school safety agent suddenly ran past me. From previous experience, I knew that meant students were fighting. I began running behind him. We pushed through the throngs of students to separate the combatants.

Before the crowd was dispersed, I heard over an agent's radio, "Eighty-five at the main!"

Eighty-five was code for a fight. I ran along with agents and students to the main entrance of the school. Before this fight was under control, I heard another eighty-five called on the second floor. I decided not to run to that one. At this time, my head was spinning. I was mentally and physically exhausted. All eyes were on me. It was as if they were saying, "Welcome to Beach Channel. Do you know what you got into?"

I decided to get away from the madness and went to my office. I dropped in my chair, put both of my hands over my face, and said aloud, "What the hell is going on? This is crazy."

I felt lonely. I could not call any colleagues for advice. All high school principals were on the retreat. "It's lonely at the top" really meant something to me that day. After chasing a fight or two after that, the day did end. I thanked God.

During my first two months at Beach Channel, I ran around the building trying to resolve every conceivable situation. Too much was happening. Fire alarms were pulled three to five times a day.

One assistant principal would get on the PA system and interrupt instruction without hesitation.

"Mr. S., please report to room 222 for your coverage. The students are waiting for you."

"Ms. Q., we found your keys."

Five minutes later, I would hear, "Student X, report to the dean's office."

This went on and on. Fights ... Police ... EMS ... Fights ... Police ... EMS ... Accidents ... Fights ... EMS. It was a mess.

In the midst of all this chaos, we had teachers who wanted to teach and students who wanted to learn. The majority of the staff and students wanted discipline and safety. They lacked effective leadership. Staff had lost confidence in the administration. Parents felt disconnected. Students felt disconnected, disrespected, and unsafe. For the most part, the school functioned as an island unto itself. The surrounding communities had abandoned the school. Local parents who were more affluent or involved chose other schools outside of their community. Under similar circumstances, I would have done the same.

I observed and listened for about two months, which was the remainder of the school year. I did not come in and begin changing things, even the things that were obviously not working. Any sporadic action I might have taken would have been like placing a finger in a hole in a dike. The water would have just escaped through another hole. From the beginning, I realized it would take a team of committed adults to begin the school's needed transformation.

I led by example. I did not expect anything from anyone that I would not do myself. I continually walked the halls all day long. I did not stop. I was inside, outside, up the block, and down the block. I went around the school's perimeter. I was everywhere. I observed everything as I began formulating a plan of action. Here's what I realized:

Beach Channel had too many rules. They were not consistently enforced. The consequences for breaking rules depended on the particular staff member handling the situation. Among the many superfluous rules, teachers were encouraged to lock the classroom doors immediately following the late bell. This policy obviously contributed to the hallway traffic. The administration did periodic hallway sweeps. Sweeps were an attempt to gather all students who were cutting and bring them to a particular location, the auditorium. It was the only place that could hold the large number of students who were late or chose to cut class.

An assigned school aide began to call parents while the students socialized in the auditorium. Out of the hundred or so students, the aide would get to contact maybe five to ten parents. In many cases, contact numbers were no longer connected. At the end of the period, the students would be released from the auditorium. The process would start all over again. The practice of sweeping was an effort in futility. The number of students cutting classes any given period overwhelmed the process. I was puzzled that, even though the policy obviously did not work, the previous administration continued it. The rules contributed to the chaos.

The school environment was so out of control during my first few months. The thought of observing instruction was not paramount. I had to figure out a way to control the fighting, the intruders, the cutting, the robberies, and the assaults. I had to control the madness. One problem was dealing with people's expectations. Some expected immediate change; others did not have any expectations at all. "It has been this way, and it will always be this way." I had already concluded that the school rules were contributing to the problem.

So, I decided to revise the rules. There was no time to do this by committee, as some may have suggested. These rules needed to be in place by September. Instead of some lengthy document, I decided on thirteen basic rules. Here are several examples:

1. Carry your program card and Student ID at all times. It must be shown upon request of any staff member. Your ID card cannot be altered or defaced.
2. Students are required to carry a pass when not in a classroom. It must be shown upon request.
3. Smoking, gambling, and the use of alcohol or drugs are prohibited as well as possession of mace or other dangerous chemical substances.
4. Beepers and cellular phones are prohibited in the building. Possession of these items will lead to confiscation. Radios, cassettes, and or Walkmans many not be played or seen in the building. All confiscated items may be returned to parents one week after confiscation, during evening hours.
5. Appropriate dress is expected of everyone. Any student, either male or female, may not wear hats or scarves in school. Warm weather dress should be discrete.
6. Fighting/being involved in a fight will lead to disciplinary action, for example, suspension or arrest.

Before I would discipline a student, I asked if he or she was aware a rule had been broken. Unbelievably, some were not. I knew, if students were aware, they would be able to accept the consequences, as long as they saw the rules being applied consistently and equally to all. Contradictory adult behavior had been a major problem for students in the past. For example, students were told not to eat in class. Yet, the school administration gave them just about every opportunity to buy junk food or bagels throughout the day. While one adult sold the food, another said they couldn't eat it. Talk about madness! Once we began applying the rules consistently and fairly, things began to slowly improve. To paraphrase a proverb, the wheels of change grind exceedingly slow. I also removed the vending machines from the hallways and closed the bagel shop.

After about the second month of the new school year, I could begin turning my attention to instruction. Until this point, assistant principals were running their departments with little or no input from me. I was so busy trying to put out "fires" that it was difficult, if not impossible, for me to focus on instructional concerns. This changed on October 9, 1997. Carol Gresser, then Queens member of the board of education, and John Lee, my superintendent, visited. Here's part of the observation letter he wrote to me on October 15:

We then toured the school, and you are to be commended for your positive rapport with your students and staff. You also indicated you have begun teaching an occasional class when teachers are absent as a way of modeling for your teachers and keeping in touch with what is happening in the classroom. During our tour, you stopped several students to question why they were in the hallways. At one point, when you observed a student was wearing a hat, you walked into a classroom and removed the student's hat.

Some of the issues I discussed with you after Ms. Gresser left included the following:

1. We observed a teacher who was seated while teaching. Ms. Gresser expressed her dismay at this. It is important you remind the assistant principals and teachers that teachers should not be seated but should be on their feet and actively teaching their lessons.

2. Many of the doors to classrooms were closed and actually locked. You indicated the history is that teachers felt that because of the lack of control in the hallways and other safety issues, they were accustomed to locking their classroom doors. We agreed this is one of the areas that you will begin to work on with your faculty to get them to feel comfortable to teach with their classroom doors open. You indicated you made a commitment to the teachers that you would work to restore order in the hallways and in fact you have moved in this direction. Now we need the teachers to open up their doors.

3. In addition, many of the windows on the doors were completely covered by paper or posters, blocking any view in or out of the classroom. Please direct your staff to remove this immediately. It is a safety issue, both for the students and the staff.

The letter continued to provide a few more recommendations. I needed this visit. I agreed one hundred percent with the superintendent's observation. I did believe we had made a tremendous amount of progress in four months. Nevertheless, his critique motivated me.

I moved forward. I addressed some rules and practices about teacher behavior. They could no longer lock out students after the late bell. They had to remove the paper that covered the windows on the classroom doors. All were signs that told students, "You are not welcomed." I made the following commitment to them. "When you open your doors, I will get the students in." Getting them in the classroom was the first task. I also asked teachers to stand outside their classroom doors during student passing and to stand when they teach. I regret that my expectations of teachers could not be requirements. Their contract protected them from certain requirements, such as standing in the classroom doorway during passing. A supervisor could only make such a request. Fortunately, we had about seventy percent of teachers who acted in the best interest of students.

Outside of all rules, regulations, and procedures for teachers, my most important task was to get them to teach. For many of the teachers, this was not a simple task. The school environment had become so chaotic. It must be told that a small number of teachers relished the fact that things were out of control. When schools are chaotic, no one is "watching the store." In other words, no one is monitoring instruction. Fortunately for students at Beach Channel, dedicated teachers and staff managed to work within their stormy surroundings.

Discipline with compassion was the cornerstone of my approach. This means I wanted everyone to understand why they were being disciplined. I explained to students why they were being suspended, "You cannot hurt people with impunity."

I explained to teachers why they were receiving an unsatisfactory rating. For some, this was new.

During a post-observation conference, I asked a teacher, "How do you think the lesson went?"

He said, "I did not seem to connect with the students. They did not understand what I was trying to explain to them." Basically, he described his lesson as unsatisfactory.

I concluded the meeting with, "For all of the reasons we discussed and agreed on, you will receive an unsatisfactory for this lesson." If looks could kill ... He could not believe it. I could not believe he could not believe it. I came to understand he had performed that way since being in the school. He never received an unsatisfactory rating. Not much was expected of this teacher and others.

Likewise, not much was expected of the students. Even worse, some students did not expect anything of themselves. A large number of students were completely demoralized by the time they reached high school. They had been yelled at and threatened with failure. In fact, they had built a resistance to the threat of failure. Even worse, some had to come to expect it.

A student would be commonly asked, "How did you do with your classes this marking period?"

They would readily reply, "I only failed three."

"How can you say you *only* failed three?"

"Last marking period, I failed everything." That was perspective.

Two months after the superintendent's visit to Beach Channel, I received the following letter from a teacher:*

> *Dear Mr. Gassaway,*
>
> *I know teachers rarely write complimentary letters to principals, but I felt I had to say this. Whatever you are doing is working. It is a nice feeling to be able to keep the doors to my classroom open. The tone of the school has definitely changed since you took charge. I just thought you should know there are teachers who appreciate what you have done to give us a nice environment to teach in.*
>
> *Sincerely,*
> *XXXXXXX*

*The letter was dated December 19, 1997.

On October 14, 1998, one year after becoming principal of Beach Channel, I received word that I was selected as a "Title I Distinguished Educator" by the New York State Education Department in collaboration with the New York City Board of Education. People were beginning to hear about the good things that were happening at Beach Channel. I was very proud of our students and staff. We had some dynamic staff members who worked hard without any kind of recognition. They were committed to the children long before I arrived on that rainy Friday.

Our efforts also received some much needed positive press from the local newspaper in the area, the *Rockaway Wave*. Positive press helps to get the word out about the school. The *Rockaway Wave* printed the following editorial in a January 15, 2000, issue of their weekly publication:

Beach Channel's Comeback

It took leadership. It took vision. It took courage. These ingredients were combined to return Beach Channel High School to its heyday, a school Rockawayites could be proud of. Leading this charge, with a group of dedicated and determined teachers, was Bernard Gassaway, the principal of Beach Channel.

Let's rewind back a few years and take a look at what Beach Channel looked like. Parents were afraid to send their kids to the school because of "safety" concerns. Students would hang out in front of the school all hours of the day, often leading to fights. Teacher morale and school spirit was low. There were principals who said they were in charge, but they spent more time behind closed doors or away at meetings. That has changed under the leadership of Gassaway, whose hands-on approach is refreshing and necessary.

Fast forward to the present and you'll see the changes are dramatic. Drive by anytime and, except for the normal hours that students enter and leave school, you will not see any kids hanging around the premises. Inside the school is where the real improvements have taken place. Students aren't roaming the hallways, but in the classrooms learning. Beach Channel's teachers are excited about teaching and students are excited about learning.

Now there is no excuse for parents to take their kids out of the district for a "better" high school. Beach Channel is that "better" high school. The creation of the Beach Channel Law Institute, with an actual courtroom, is just one more bonus. Beach Channel has a well-respected Oceanography Institute, Honors Institute, Business Institute and a handful of other specialized programs.

Gassaway and his team of administrators and teachers have done a great job in turning the school around. Active parents who have worked close with administrators to accomplish these achievements must not be forgotten for their dedication. There are challenges still ahead of the school, but with the same leadership, vision and courage as displayed in the past two years, Beach Channel will not only be a shining star in Rockaway, but a shining a shining star throughout the city.

By far, the most important thing you can do to help turn around any school is ensure a competent, trained teacher is in every classroom. Equally important, the teachers and other staff must be caring individuals. I would be the first to go to war for good teachers. They should be compensated for the God-like work they perform daily. However, too many incompetent teachers should never see the light of day in a classroom. A teacher is like a brain surgeon. Would you want an incompetent brain surgeon operating on you or your child?

I will be the first to admit that Beach Channel continued struggling with some of the issues that I found when I arrived. However, no one would argue that we made a significant difference in the quality of life for the entire school community.

Here are some of the strategies that contributed to what I call the "Beach Channel Renaissance." We:

- Established achievable goals.
- Established sound policies and disseminated them frequently. A known policy is more likely to be followed than an unknown policy.
- Held monthly assembly programs. They were instructional, informational, and extracurricular.
- Invested in staff development.
- Rewarded success. We thought of multiple ways to praise and reward desired behaviors.
- Praised and rewarded staff who performed well and beyond the call of duty.
- Anticipated the ebbs and flows (before and after holidays).
- Provided staff with the tools to get the job done.
- Conducted frequent, constructive inspection of instruction.
- Embraced parents as partners.
- Established a responsive discipline program. Staff and students realized that inappropriate behavior would not be tolerated.
- Gave initiatives a chance to work.
- Publicized successes. We wrote frequent press releases.
- Replicated programs and practices that worked at effective schools.
- Empowered students.
- Responded to safety concerns.
- Engaged students and staff in community service.

Principal's Diary

August 28, 2000 (first day after short summer vacation)

I was pulled out of the building today for an 11:00 AM principal's meeting with the superintendent. I do not understand why we are pulled from our building during this time. We need to plan with our leadership team.

I attended a PTA Executive Board Meeting at 7:00 PM. We scheduled another parent meeting to coincide with the PTA meeting to boost attendance at the meeting. Between fifteen and twenty parents would generally attend these meetings.

August 29, 2000

I was pulled out of the building for an all-day principal's retreat. As I sat at these retreats, my mind would be back at the school. I thought retreats were basically a waste of time and money.

August 30, 2000

I was pulled out again to attend a meeting at 9:00 AM. This was a College Now Meeting at La Guardia College.*

August 31, 2000

On the fourth day of the school year, I got to spend the entire day in the building. I spent this day interviewing staff. The district superintendent's office sent candidates to the school. We were expected to accept anyone they sent, sight unseen. I asked one candidate why he wanted to leave his current position with a college to teach high school science. He said, "For the money." I abruptly ended the interview and told him to leave my office ("Get out!"). He looked surprised. Ten minutes later, I received a telephone call from the district office telling me I had to accept this teacher. I held my ground and said, "There is no way this individual would ever work at Beach Channel." They did not force the issue that time.

The remainder of my day was spent meeting with the programmer, custodian, and assistant principals.

September 1, 2000

We held our freshmen orientation. We had more than 1,000 people in the school.

September 5, 2000

Teachers returned from summer vacation. We brought in seniors and juniors to pick up program cards and make program changes, if needed. This would help ensure a smooth school opening.

---

*College Now was a special program being introduced to the school. Basically, it was a cohort of ninth graders who would receive special programming and intensive college preparation.

September 6, 2000

We brought in sophomores and freshmen to pick up programs and make program changes, if needed.

We conducted staff development activities for teachers. Teachers and outside consultants generally led these workshops.

September 7, 2000

This was the first full day of instruction. All of our planning would be put to the test.

The day included program changes, class changes for teachers, as well as parents trying to register or transfer their children. It was a very busy time.

One parent called and wanted her child to pick up her little brother from the junior high school across the street. The same parent reported her daughter was having a problem with a girl in her class. She wanted her daughter's class changed. According to the parent, the two girls had problems in their previous school. The parents even had problems with each other when they were students. Damn! This sounds so familiar. I suggested mediation. The parent said they tried it in junior high school. It had failed.

At the end of the day, I received a call from another parent. Her child had not made it home. I suggested the parent wait for another hour and call back. She did not call; I called her. The child made it home. She missed her bus or decided to chill with her friends. "Welcome to high school."

September 8, 2000

I arrived to work at 5:55 AM to do paperwork.

An "A-Typical" Day as Principal

3:30 AM	Awake between 2:30 AM and 3:30 AM.
5:45	Arrive to work.
5:50	Review e-mail.
	Read online newspapers for education-related articles.
6:15	Walk through entire building with pad in hand.
	Try to get the pulse of building.
6:40	Return to office.
	Take and return phone calls from day before.
7:10–8:25	Say "good morning" to students at student entrance.
	Begin to get the pulse from observing students.
8:30	Stop by office to say "good morning" to secretary.
	Ask about any appointments.
8:30–9:00	Walk the building.

	Informally observe classes.
	Talk to security officers and ask what's happening. Security often hears things from students during entry.
9:00–10:00	Deal with numerous unplanned issues.
	Meet with parents and students. These meetings are generally not planned or scheduled. I schedule the majority of my meetings after school.
10:00–12:00	Formally observe two classes (full periods).
12:00–1:00	Visit student cafeteria.
	Visit dean's office.
1:00–2:00	Walk the building.
	Handle situations as they occur.
	Troubleshoot.
	Feel the pulse of building.
	Talk to staff in the hallways or in their classrooms. Ask about their day.
2:15	Return to my office to check for messages.
	Return a few urgent calls.
2:25–2:45	Go out for student dismissal.
	Talk to students.
	Observe students as they get on school buses or walk to train stations.
	As buses pull away, walk toward the train station to monitor student safety.
2:50	Return to the building.
	Sit in my office with door open. This is a signal for students and staff to enter.
4:00	Meet with parents and students. Generally, these are suspension hearings.
4:30	Meet with community-based organizations.

5:00	Attend a leadership meeting or basketball, volleyball, soccer game, or other after-school function.
6:00	Return to office to do paperwork. Debrief with key staff.
8:00 PM	Leave to go home.

A Day in the Life of an Urban High School Principal

Have you heard the joke, "If you want to make God laugh, tell him your plans?" God had many laughs on me. Despite my effort to plan each day, something unexpected would come up that would require that I change them.

For example, I was scheduled to observe an English teacher's lesson one day. With writing pad in hand, my secretary said a student would like to talk to me. This was a frequent occurrence. I was very accessible, so such a request was not unusual. Once a student took the initiative to approach me with a problem, I would rarely turn him or her away. This particular student just had an argument with another student at the train station near the school. She wanted to inform me that the conflict was probably going to continue in school. This was her indirect way of asking me to intervene. Students rarely come straight out and request help.

As was my way, I called the other student to my office to person-ally mediate this conflict. Even though I had faith in my deans, this student did not. That's why she came to me. I was reluctant to pass a problem to another staff member. Students often approached me because they knew I would listen to them without prejudice. Although they did not always agree with my decision, they usually respected it.

During this mediation between the two students, I explained the ground rules. I asked each student to address me when telling her side of the story. I also insisted that both speak softly and slowly. I wanted each of the students to hear one another. The basis for their argument was over a "he said, she said" scenario. They real-ized their argument was baseless once they were able to get their stories heard. My mission was accomplished. I prevented two students from what may have been another traumatic experience in school.

I realized my approach to working with students required a lot of my time. If a student came to me with a problem, unless I could not handle it, I did not believe in passing it on. I owned the problem. On countless instances, students would say, "I tried to tell so-and-so (an adult) that he was bothering me." I would say to myself, "The adult dropped the ball." I did not want any children to suffer because of an adult's negligence or failure to respond appropriately. Students deserved peace, especially in school.

Foreign Impression—
A Letter from an Intern

January 20, 2001

Mr. Bernard Gassaway, Principal

Beach Channel High School

100-00 Beach Channel Drive

Rockaway Park, NY 11694

Dear Mr. Gassaway:

My name is Myriam P. I am a French student working on my masters in sciences of education in Bordeaux, France. I came to New York City to observe the American educational system and compare different schools. I started in Beach Channel High School, and it was my very best experience. I felt so comfortable in this school because the message from the principal and assistant principals is clear. I can use two keywords: discipline and collaboration.

Discipline in each classroom is firmly done by teachers, and Mr. Monereau puts all his energy to keep a peaceful setting in this school.

Collaboration with Mr. Gassaway, Mr. Monereau, and all the staff is efficient. I was impressed to see the fantastic organization. In the hall, when we meet a student, we can always know what he is doing there and what room he belongs to. It is the only school where I have seen such strict discipline. I had the opportunity to assist different meetings. I could see how seriously they take their jobs. The doors were opened. I was free to go everywhere without any restriction. I could observe classes, interview teachers, and take pictures. It was not the case in the other schools where I went. Here, there is nothing to hide!

The environment is safe. The school is so beautiful with the bay all around. Students and teachers decorate the walls, exactly like a private school. It's just great to walk in the school and see all these colors. We can feel the enthusiastic atmosphere Mr. Gassaway wants to create here.

I observed many classes. I have to say the classroom management is very efficient. I explained to the other teachers I met in the other schools how organized the classes were at Beach Channel High School. Some took the idea and later told me that it works. They try to follow the example of Beach Channel, especially by writing the aim, due now, and homework on the board. This was not done before in their schools.

Yes, this is a public school. Mr. Gassaway and Mr. Monereau can be proud of what they are doing. Who says there is no great public high school in New York City? I have to add that some people in France and elsewhere think students in American public high schools are wild and disrespectful. This is not the case at Beach Channel High School.

They are spontaneous. They always told me, "Hi." I never felt so insecure among them. They never pushed me in the halls. We don't have to be afraid of them. In some schools, teachers are frightened. Here, I could observe a special relationship with students and teachers.

I am very happy to have had the opportunity to observe Beach Channel High School. When people live in other countries, they usually hear more negative things about American public schools than positive ones. I now know it is not always so. The positiveness of Beach Channel High School will remain in my heart. Wherever I go, I will always talk about it! I have concluded that it really takes great leaders who are compassionate and dedicated to make a school what it should be. Students are watching, and they know when the principal cares. I am happy to say that Mr. Gassaway is a very concerned principal. As a result, the school is well-organized. Students learn better. Teachers are more motivated to teach. At Beach Channel High School, I have seen everything that is positive in the public school system.

Sincerely,

M.P.

Bomb Threat

The unfortunate reality is that there is nothing new about bomb threats in the lives of urban high school principals. After September 11, 2001, I know we experienced an increase in threats at Beach Channel.

I was going about my daily routine one day when my secretary discretely informed me that we received another bomb threat. As with previous bomb threats, we followed our bomb threat protocol. After making the obligatory calls to the police and the superintendent's office, I assessed the legitimacy of the threat. I had to make a decision within three to five minutes. Evacuate, or dismiss the threat as a hoax. What if I make the wrong decision? I could hear all of the Monday morning quarterbacks in my ear, "He should have evacuated. He received a call. Why didn't he evacuate? He should be fired."

In reality, it is not a simple decision to evacuate 2,500 staff and students. This was one of those decisions that a committee could not make. The final decision rested with one individual, the principal. Even though the police department had the authority to overrule my decision, they never did.

I remained focused because I knew what was at stake, the lives of my students and staff. The individual who called in the bomb threat sounded like a teenager. He did not give a time for the bomb to explode. There were no suspicious items found. Police did not mandate an evacuation, so I decided not to evacuate the building.

Shortly after I decided to proceed with business as usual, school safety informed me that 600 to 800 students and staff from the middle school across the street were outside of our auditorium. They were waiting to get in. They received a bomb threat moments after we received one. They decided to evacuate. As fate would have it, Beach Channel was a backup location for their school in case of such an emergency. I immediately decided to open our auditorium for the evacuated students. However, I informed them that we also received a threat. They decided to follow the script. They filed into the auditorium. I assigned my assistant principal of security to assist them with this evacuation. We also went into contingency mode. We may need to serve them lunch and provide access to telephones to call parents. Of course, the irony did not escape me. We both undoubtedly received the threats from the same individual. I decided not to evacuate; they decided to evacuate. By taking this school into my building, I nearly doubled my responsibility. The bottom line is that a decision had to be made. I made it, and I thank God I am here to tell you about it.

God Bless You

In January 2002, controversy erupted at Beach Channel. An age-old constitutional issue, separation of church and state, confronted us. The issue was our school marquee that read, "God Bless You."

It began shortly after September 11, 2001. Our PTA maintained the school sign. To demonstrate support for our country, they decided to put a sign that read "God Bless America." Patriotism was running high in the country. No one was going to publicly argue that such a sign should be removed. After several months passed, it came time for the PTA to add information about testing and meetings to the sign. "God Bless America" could no longer fit in the available space. However, "God Bless You" had just the right number of letters to fit. So, they went with that phrase to continue in the spirit of remembering the tragic event.

According to the school-based United Federation of Teacher's representative, a small number of staff questioned the PTA's right to post such a sign. I did not have any objection to the sign. I suggested to the representative that he feel free to contact board of education officials to get a ruling from them. He did. Meanwhile the PTA updated the sign again. This time, they removed the saying altogether, without regard to any pending decision from the New York City Board of Education.

On January 24, 2002, roughly three weeks after the PTA voluntarily removed the sign, a board of education spokesperson was quoted in the *New York Post* article entitled "No Sign of God at QNS. School." This spokesperson implied that I was ordered to take down the sign because it violated the United States constitution. However, they had no problem with the initial sign, "God Bless America" because it was patriotic and no one complained. Not to argue a belated point, but "God" was the operative word. If you objected based on constitutional grounds, that is, separation of church and state, then both signs would be a violation.

What angered the PTA members and I was the board of education's blatant lie that I was ordered to take the sign down. In fact, they never issued a written or verbal ruling to me. In their typical fashion, they tested the political wind and decided to take the path of least resistance. At the time, I realized that people who represent systems would do just about anything to protect that system. Lying was par for the course.

More frightening than the lies of the board of education officials was the public's reaction to the misinformation. Look at some excerpts of e-mails that I received from all over the country regarding my alleged actions:

Would "Mohammed Condemns America" be more appropriate? I am not a religious person. I am, however, outraged by the decision to remove the "God Bless America" sign from the front of your students' school.

"God Bless America" has become a symbol of the mind-set that brought you into a position such as you have. Freedom, reward for hard work, and recognition that work ethics bring rewards. Our American way of life pays for your damn salary. To hell with those who attempt to bring us down. Now your "politically correct gotta cover my ass and not piss anybody off" lack of fortitude will bring your sorry asses to the forefront of discussion. To hell with you and others like you. I will enjoy watching your public humiliation.

Once again, one person gripes, and everyone cowers and runs into the corner. Shame on you for removing the sign! I guess you've never looked at your money, issued by the United States government, that says, "In God We Trust." How quickly you forget Sept. 11 and Nov. 12!

Hello:

As a concerned citizen and taxpayer, I wanted to express my concern over your poor judgment in removing the "God Bless You" sign at your school. Let me say first that giving in to the 'separation of church and state' argument was your first display of poor judgment. If you had any true legal expertise whatsoever, you would very quickly realize there is not the slightest of legal arguments here. What's really important here is the horrible example you have just set for our youth! [sic]

I relate this story to illustrate that a simple act of kindness can potentially turn into a constitutional or religious battle. I learned a valuable lesson. You cannot control what the press prints. You also cannot control people's reaction to what they read in the press.

School Fortress

Metal detectors are a reality for many children in urban high schools. Some schools have stationary metal detectors that are used daily. Others, like Beach Channel, have random scanning. This meant my students were subjected to scanning at least once a week. School safety agents used handheld wands to scan each student. X-ray machines, like the ones used in airports, were used to inspect student backpacks and belongings.

I have always opposed scanning despite the fact that weapons would be periodically found on students. The weapon of choice was a box cutter. Once a student was found with a box cutter, he or she would claim it was used for an after-school job. In reality, the majority carried box cutters for protection.

Scanning had an affect on me as well as on my students. I became tense when I realized scanning would take place. I knew precisely how students would react. They became stressed. In fact, an analysis would probably show that more student fights occurred on scanning days. Students expressed that they felt the school safety agents were violating them. It often came down to the manner in which the agents spoke to the students, usually in disrespectful tones. Even though we assigned school personnel to observe the scanning process, it did not lessen the tension between the scanning agents and the students. The scanning agents were part of a traveling scanning crew. They did not know the students, and the students did not know them. As crazy as it may sound, students were more likely to accept disrespect from someone they knew than from a stranger.

I fully empathized with my students. It is easier to get into an airport than get into some schools. Truth be told, it is easier to visit a loved one in prison than get into certain schools. Even as a principal, when I visited other schools, I was subjected to scanning. It was humiliating and degrading.

One day during scanning at Beach Channel, I heard "code blue" over the radio, the code for a knife. A student apparently entered the building and was caught with a knife approximately eight inches in length. The police officer assigned to the school arrested this student. Within thirty minutes, the boy's grandmother came in to see me. Even though she appeared to be upset with me, I think she was fed up with her grandson. She demanded to know why he was arrested.

I said, "He brought a knife to school."

"Well," she said, "then somebody was bothering him. When I go to the precinct, I will fight them."

I advised her against this action, but she left as quickly as she came. On a day like this, it would be hard to argue against scanning.

I think there can be a middle ground as far as schools using metal detection as a safety measure. If metal detectors and scanners must be used, the scanning agents should be required to receive ongoing sensitivity training. Students often get into confrontations with security agents during scanning because they feel disrespected. From personal experience, I know it takes a lot to swallow your pride once you have been disrespected.

School safety agents are the backbone of many urban high schools. They have earned the respect of students and staff. They take their job seriously. However, some agents are simply nasty, angry individuals. They should be removed from children.

Sexual Abuse

Regardless of what form it takes, sexual abuse is horrible. So, when I was accused of ignoring a child's allegation of sexual harassment by a teacher, I was surprised and disappointed.

One morning, I was standing outside of the school to greet students, as was my routine, when a female student handed me a flyer.

She said, "Mr. Gassaway, look at what this lady is handing out at the train station." The majority of my students took this train to school.

The flyer read:

> *Are you, the female students of Beach Channel High School, aware a teacher on staff sexually harassed a fourteen-year-old freshman? Are you aware that Mr. Gassaway will not speak to the parents of the students and he will not dismiss the teacher? Are you aware that another teacher has*

helped to harass this student and her parents?*

Be careful, ladies. This teacher's next victim could be you! Have your parents call Mr. Gassaway to complain about what this teacher is getting away with. Organize as students, and have a formal strike. Refuse to work in a school that allows the sexual harassment of women! Demand that student government take a stand for the women at Beach Channel High School, even if Mr. Gassaway won't. By refusing to cooperate, Mr. Gassaway is sending the message to female students that he believes in sexual harassment and is disrespectful of women in the Beach Channel building.

After having someone identify the individual distributing the flyer as the parent of the student accuser, I asked myself, "I wonder why she's doing that?"

In fact, I had responded to her child's allegation by following protocol. The matter was being investigated. When I met with the parent, she denied any knowledge of the flyer I presented to her. From that moment, I knew nothing I could say would matter to this individual. I notified the superintendent's office of the flyer. I decided to go about my day and deal with any fallout as it occurred.

I did not receive any phones calls from parents. They did not believe it. Students ignored her call for protest. They expressed empathy for me, "That's not right what that lady is saying about you. We got your back."

When this parent realized her approach did not yield any results, she disappeared. Her daughter also stopped coming to school. I actually felt sorry for her child. I thought she would be scarred for life, regardless of the veracity of her allegation. This particular allegation of teacher sexual harassment was unsubstantiated.

*The actual teacher and office were mentioned.

In another case, I was baffled when a school safety agent decided to clear his conscience with me.

He said, "Mr. Gassaway, I think it's wrong for an agent to have a relationship with a former student."

The student had graduated the previous year. Upon receiving this information, I reported it to the appropriate authorities. They ruled that nothing could be done to this officer. There was no proof that their relationship began when this young lady was a student. I felt the school safety division wanted to avoid this potentially embarrassing situation. The division of school safety later promoted this particular safety agent. However, one year later, he was terminated for an unrelated event.

Unfortunately, during a few incidents, students were manipulated into relationships with staff. I always felt partially responsible for anyone who may have been hurt under my leadership.

I asked myself a series of questions, "How could this have happened? What could I have done to prevent it? Did I miss any signs?"

Here is some advice for my colleagues: If it feels or looks as if a staff member and students are too close for comfort, err on the side of protecting the student. Report it to the investigators. Also, regardless of what some school officials may tell you, inform the parents. They have a right to know of any allegations of child abuse in any form, just as we have an obligation to inform authorities if we suspect parents of child abuse.

Also, make it a point to remind all staff that it is not okay to have sexual relations with students. It is illegal, immoral, and reprehensible.

Celebrate Success

As a teacher, my most memorable days at Boys and Girls High School were the honor roll celebrations. Legendary principal Frank Mickens strongly believed children needed to be celebrated as often as possible. He believed success could be contagious. He held at least three honor roll celebrations a year. These were huge productions. These were different from normal school celebrations because they were held after school, during the early evening, or on the weekend.

When I arrived at Beach Channel, I noticed the current regime also believed in honoring students. They followed the routine practice of recognizing students during assembly programs. Assemblies were generally scheduled to begin between 11:00 AM and 1:00 PM. This format did not seem to work for several reasons:

- Award recipients would shy away from public recognition because they were among a minority of students to receive awards.

- Disinterested students who were not receiving awards were compelled to attend these assemblies. The noise from the nonparticipatory observers was so loud that you could not hear the name of the recipient being called.
- Parents generally did not attend.

Sometime during my first year as principal, I decided we would move our student recognition assemblies to evenings. This concept received some resistance. I never let opposition sway me from what I strongly believed was a winner. After all, I had experienced success with this type of function.

We asked teachers and administrators to volunteer to attend our first evening honor roll assembly. We ordered refreshments. Each awardee received a certificate and T-shirt that read, "I Am an Honor Roll Student." The T-shirt idea was another concept I took from Boys and Girls.

Our first evening assembly was a huge success. Nearly 300 parents, friends, and relatives attended. The event was straightforward. We had three categories: gold, silver, and bronze. I watched students proudly walk through the school halls with their shirts on parade. The shirts did wonders for school spirit.

Each year, this program grew. We went from roughly 100 award recipients to nearly 500. We eventually conducted two honor roll programs a year: one in late October for the June honor students and one in March for the January honor students. We gave out T-shirts, televisions, money, and other exciting gifts. We gave each parent a free raffle upon entry. They could win cash prizes, televisions, or other electronic devices. Our audiences eventually grew to more than 1,000 people, students, and their guests. Once we established our band and gospel choir, they performed at these events. It was like a music concert. The spotlight was shone on students as they approached the stage. A projector flashed the pictures of the gold and silver recipients as their name was called. The audience went wild with excitement.

It was their Oscar night. We threw parties for the them. The parents of these students generally would not allow them to attend neighborhood parties. Our parties allowed them to have fun in a safe environment. All it took for the students to rush to the dance floor was to play any of 2 Live Crew's songs. "Pop That Coochie" and "Do Do Brown" were among their favorites.

Thanksgiving
Senior Citizen Dinner

One day during my second year as principal of Beach Channel, I introduced the idea of the school having a Thanksgiving Day dinner program for local senior citizens. I took the idea to host a senior citizen dinner from my days as a high school teacher. I remember the hordes of student and staff volunteers. It was a very special day that did wonders for the participants and the guests. It was a win-win situation.

I wanted to have the dinner on Thanksgiving Day. Most adults expressed reservations. They said students would not volunteer on that day because they wanted to be with their families. I reflected on my childhood Thanksgivings. We would begin eating at 10:00 AM. I never remember having a formal sit-down dinner. After we ate, the day was boring. Making a leap, I figured many of my students had similar experiences, so I did not heed the warning. We moved forward with our plans to do the dinner on Thanksgiving Day. We asked for monetary donations, food, and supplies. The response was overwhelming. We asked the school's cafeteria staff to assist. They needed permission from their administration to approve overtime. After I lobbied a few officials, permission was granted. In the days leading up to the event, we put out a call over the PA system to ask for volunteers. Students and staff began signing up. It appeared to be moving slowly. On the day before the event, after school finished and many staff and students began leaving to begin the long holiday weekend, a few of us went to the gymnasium to set up. To my surprise, about ten students were waiting for me when I arrived. Before the evening was complete, about thirty student and staff volunteers had arrived, just for the setup. I was so pleased.

The morning of Thanksgiving Day came. I arrived to school around 7:30 AM. Traci, Atiya, students, and staff began arriving shortly after. The dinner was scheduled to run from 11:00 AM to 2:00 PM. At approximately 10:30 AM, the first senior citizen, a male gentleman, arrived. By this time, we had nearly seventy-five student volunteers who welcomed this gentleman. Then our first bus filled with senior citizens arrived. It was a sight to see. A line of seniors were on parade with their walkers, canes, and wheelchairs. Student volunteers were so happy. I was quietly overjoyed because I knew it was an immediate success. After the seniors were seated, students and staff came to their tables to take orders. The operation ran smoothly. One person took food orders; another took drink orders. The day was made extra special when I saw students and staff working together. If anything was true, the students ran the show. I simply observed with a joyful heart. The power of giving cannot be overstated. Students were falling over one another to serve people. Some of the students who had caused conflict in the school leading up to this event were the most enthusiastic. I did not hesitate to welcome their participation. This event changed people, including our guests, students, and staff.

After the seniors citizens finished eating, the music began. That first year, we had a DJ, DJ Holla, Donnell Holmes from Edgemere, Far Rockaway. It was amazing to see them on the dance floor. We were told one gentleman had a pacemaker. The attendant from his home had to tell him to slow down. I knew this event was good for his heart and soul.

The agility and flexibility of the seniors surprised the students. They were not shy about strutting on the dance floor. The following letters from three of the participants captures the essence of the event:

Dear Family and Friends of BCHS,

We are thankful for the student body, staff, and families who reached out to make a difference in our Rockaway Community. When everyone is busy celebrating the holidays, the BCHS family invited Hammells Senior Center and other groups for an unforgettable Thanksgiving luncheon.

We were greeted at the door and escorted to our festively decorated tables with balloons and falling leaves centerpieces, which surrounded the dance floor. Friendly, family-like respect was illustrated by the students, staff, and PTA members. We felt like we were at home.

The luncheon of various appetizers of choice, turkey, sweet potatoes, cranberry sauce, vegetables, salad, breads of all kinds, beverages of choice, including the traditional apple cider, and desserts of numerous kinds was served with love.

When we couldn't eat another mouthful, the famous BCHS band lead by Mr. Domfort came marching in and played every kind of musical selection from jitterbug, disco, salsa, waltzes, electric slide, and the Macarena. What made it even more enjoyable and unforgettable was the fact that the students asked the seniors to come and join them on the dancing floor. Assemblywoman Audrey Pheffer stopped by and joined in the festivities. Everyone danced their feet off and had a great time.

The pure spirit of giving and fellowship was illustrated by the BCHS family. We truly have a lot to be thankful for, as we carried our gift bags into the unforgettable day, knowing there was not a better place to be. Please share this letter of Thanksgiving with the BCHS family and the Rockaway Community.

Respectfully,

C. and W. [sic]

A letter from a student as a class assignment:

On Thanksgiving at Beach Channel, Mr. Gassaway gave the elders a Thanksgiving they will never forget. I also will never forget. I had a good time dancing with the older ladies. Some of them look old, but they're young in heart. At first, everything looked as if it was going good. The band was playing music, but nobody was dancing. So, Miss Curran asked me to dance. Then she told me a lady looked like she wanted to dance, so I went to ask her if she wanted to dance. And she said yes. We started to dance. Everybody started to dance right next to me, and everybody was happy. Even the students had a good time. I wished it would never end. I can't wait for the next year to see them again. I love my elders.

Signed

R.S. [sic]

This next letter was very special for me:

Nov 23, 2001

Dear Principal B. Gossoway,

I whant to thank you for one of the nicest Thanks Giving Dinner I had in 70 years of my life. I whant to thank the teacher's. (all so Tina). The students. I did not belive there is a future with children. But I Have High Hopes because of your students's. I know there is a future because of your students. Your singing choir made me feel Great.* I know a lot of work went into making Thanks Giving Diner.. But belive me it made me feel wonderful again. SO again Principal Thank you again.

With appreciation

David

P.S. All involved in making the dinner [sic]

I decided we would parlay on our success with this event and begin Saturday classes for senior citizens. We would have students teach the classes. It was also a huge success. In an April 13, 2002, article in the *Rockaway Wave* newspaper the following article appeared in the Community section:

More Than 100 Seniors Going to BC High School

Senior citizens are once again welcomed at Beach Channel High School. Beginning Saturday, April 13, senior citizens will be taught, in large part, by Beach Channel High School student volunteers. Students will use this opportunity to fulfill part of

---

*Our choir was lead by a dynamic paraprofessional, Ronald Kornegay, Jr. He passed away this year. Thank you for making a significant difference in such a short period of time. God bless you.

their community service requirements. Bernard Gassaway, the school's principal, along with his seven-year-old daughter Atiya, will also teach a class. Classes are scheduled from 10 a.m. to 12 noon, for five consecutive Saturdays.

Gassaway seeks every opportunity to bring his students together with senior citizens. He believes young people need to learn how to respect and appreciate the value of wisdom and longevity. "Although my students will teach the classes, I truly believe they will learn a great deal from the seniors," said Principal Gassaway.

Most seniors will be taught computer basics. Some will learn how to "surf" the Internet. They will also be advised on what to look for when buying a computer.

Students and staff are very excited about this latest volunteer effort. Volunteerism is not new to the students and staff of Beach Channel. In addition to various fundraisers, blood and clothing drives, the school is noted in the community for its annual Thanksgiving Day senior citizen dinner. This past year, over 300 senior citizens danced and dined with student and staff volunteers on Thanksgiving Day.

The seniors are going back to school after all these years for various reasons, ranging from wanting to learn new technology to needing to help grandchildren do their schoolwork.

Presidential Encounters

I received a call on my cell phone from one of my assistant principals, Deborah Lakoff, informing me that Beach Channel was chosen to have its band play for a special event. I was told to contact our local assemblywoman's office. I tried reaching Joann Shapiro, chief of staff for Assemblywoman Audrey Pheffer.

I was sitting in my office when the return call from Joann Shapiro came in. She informed me that Hillary Clinton's staff was looking for a school band to play at Kennedy Airport when the former first family returned to New York City after leaving Washington, DC, immediately following President Bush's inauguration. Joann recommended Beach Channel. Our band had grown over the years and enjoyed community support and support from our assemblywoman. I tried being cool while telling Joann we would love to play for the Clintons. I walked over to the band room to inform the director, Barry Domfort. I was excited about the prospect of our school playing at such an auspicious event.

To appreciate my joy, you must understand the background of the band. When I first arrived at Beach Channel, we had a quartet and very few instruments. In its not so distance past, Beach Channel had several accomplished bands. I am not sure why former Beach Channel administration decided to give the musical instruments to another New York City high school. One staff person put it this way, "If these kids cannot read books, how can they be expected to read music?"

The answer to this question came in the person of Barry Domfort. He was the Mr. Holland of Beach Channel.* Simply, he believed in all children, and they believed in him and themselves. In three years, under the leadership of Mr. Domfort, our quartet grew to become a fifty-piece band. When the announcement was made that Beach Channel was selected out of all of the New York City bands, we were proud.

I was asked, "Why Beach Channel?"

I simply said, "Why not Beach Channel?" Enough said!

With much anticipation and sleepless nights, the day (January 20, 2001) arrived. Sometime around 11:00 AM, my daughter Atiya and I made it to Kennedy Airport on that windy, cold, damp day. We waited in a disorganized, crowded line to get through a guarded gate. Expecting to have some influence because my school was playing for the president, I told the people at a separate entrance that I was the principal of Beach Channel High School.

Basically, they replied, "So what?"

After an hour of patiently waiting, Atiya and I finally got in when I decided to push our way through as others had pushed past us. We walked into an enormous hangar. I immediately connected with the band. They were enjoying a respite. Freeport High School's

---

*"Mr. Holland's Opus," was a movie about a dynamic music teacher who inspired thousands of students to appreciate music and life.

band from Long Island was also there. They played classical music. It was funny because we played music in the genre of Ike and Tina Turner's "Proud Mary" and Isaac Hayes' "Theme from Shaft." The crowd loved it. I felt so proud, and I was greatly thrilled because of the pride I saw on the faces of my children. They looked great. They played song after song as we waited for the Clintons to arrive. It was cold, but spirits were high. The students played in their band uniforms, not the warmest garments. After about two hours of waiting, the wide doors of the hangar slowly began opening. The cold, frigid winds rushed in and smacked the hell out of everyone. Snow flurries began appearing. As if on cue, the 747 plane appeared out of nowhere. The crowd began going off, clapping and cheering. The plane taxied and stopped. Within minutes, former President Clinton, Senator Hillary Clinton, and Chelsea stepped out of the plane. The crowd continued cheering and clapping. Our band began playing. The Clintons rocked to our music as they stepped to the platform. Hillary Clinton spoke first. She thanked the Freeport and Beach Channel high school bands for playing. C-SPAN broadcasted this event live.

President Clinton addressed the crowd. After the speeches, they headed toward their awaiting vehicles. The band played as throngs of fans rushed to the receiving line. Regrettably, the band members did not get to meet the former first family because they were professional and continued to play. They did get to take some cool pictures near the president's plane. This was an historic event. We, Beach Channel High School, were a part of it. It was a great day!

As fate would have it, some ten months later, I met former President Clinton at an awards ceremony. It was weird. An organization called Public Education Needs Civic Involvement in Learning (PENCIL) awarded Beach Channel with an Exemplary Partnership Award. This organization sponsors an event in New York City schools called "Principal for a Day." They invite local businesspersons to visit schools in hopes of helping schools build lasting partnerships or relationships. Two years before our recognition, our "principal for a day" introduced us to people at Southampton College. We met with Southampton personnel and developed a very healthy relationship. Our partnership was indeed exemplary.*

Because of our hard work, we were invited to a red carpet event. The program was held at New York's Hammerstein Ballroom in midtown Manhattan. Once I settled down and began sipping a ginger ale, Bill Clinton entered. I was initially reluctant to approach him because everyone swarmed him, especially the women. I found it ironic because this was on the heels of the Monica Lewinsky scandal. Of all things to think about at the moment, I thought about my mother. I thought she must be laughing at the thought of her knucklehead son being in the same room as the American president, albeit former. With this thought, I waited for the right time to approach Mr. Clinton to make an introduction. His security team looked me over. I gave them a nod, assuring them I was not an enemy about to do any harm.

I asked myself, "How do I begin this introduction? Do I say Mr. President or Mr. Former President, Bill?"

I decided to say, "Hello, Mr. President. How are you?" I then reminded him that our band had played for him and his wife in January. He indicated he had enjoyed the band. I took the opportunity to ask him if he would visit the school to speak with our students. To my surprise, he agreed.

I then asked, "How do I contact you?"

---

*John Marcus, an assistant principal at Beach Channel, was largely responsible for the success of this partnership. He worked with Michael Brophy, Associate Provost of L.I.U.'s Southampton College and Horacio Burrowes, III, the first Director of Liberty Partnership at Beach Channel.

He referred me to one of his people, and they provided the contact information. He was a man of his word. On June 13, 2002, almost seven months from that second encounter, he came to Beach Channel. He was scheduled to stay for about thirty minutes. He made one request. He said he wanted the audience to be able to ask him about anything. I looked at him.

He repeated, "Anything."

Talk about stress! I just knew someone would ask him about Monica Lewinsky.

I said to myself, "Yo, Prez, just say hello and leave. Thanks for coming."

Fortunately, no one trivialized the event by asking about that situation. He addressed global issues and September 11, 2001. He enjoyed himself so much that he stayed for two-and-a-half hours and posed for pictures with students and staff. The students were beside themselves with joy. The thought of an American president visiting their school instilled pride in them. It was a day to remember.

Parents as Partners

Very simply, parental involvement does not exist in urban schools across this country because parents are not welcomed. Administrators pay lip service to parent involvement to gain whatever funding may be attached to a given initiative. Parents are frequently described as being irate. I would describe this same parent as being frustrated and concerned about his or her child's welfare. Some school principals describe parents as being a pain in the ass.

"Who does she think she is? I'm the principal after all. I do not need her advice. I will defend my teachers even if they are wrong."

It's crazy. For parents to feel welcome in schools, they must be respected. If a school disrespects parents, the school disrespects children.

Parents will become involved if they are respected. Involvement does not mean only attending the PTA meeting. Involvement means including them in setting the agenda for the school, providing them with adequate space in the school, and accepting them as equal partners.

When I was assigned to take over as principal of Beach Channel, the former principal arranged a dinner meeting so I could meet the executive members of the PTA. At this meeting, I met the future president and vice president of the PTA, Reverends Henry and Lucille Maddox. Their son Erick was attending Beach Channel.

I mentioned this meeting because I am convinced God decided to give both Henry and Lucille Maddox a special assignment. He charged them with watching over the new principal. I thank God for all of the thousands of parents who supported me over the years. However, I have a special place in my heart for the Maddox family.

Sometime during my first year, I established a Parent Reception Center. I provided parents with a large office near the front entrance of the school. I wanted students, staff, and parents to know through my actions that parents were equal partners in their children's education. Volunteer parents staffed the office daily. Mr. and Mrs. Maddox as well as Ms. Walcott mainly covered the office.

The following letter, dated June 8, 2000, summarizes my relationship with parents:

> *Dear Mr. Gassaway,*
>
> *I'm bursting with thankfulness, and I don't really know where to start. But I just had to write this letter. First, let me thank you for always being available to meet with myself and my husband when we had questions and concerns [about our son's] education. School had always been a little difficult for [him], but, through your encouragement and concern, you gave him the strength to get through.*
>
> *In a time when many principals take on the job just to be eligible for a good pension, it is refreshing to know someone such as yourself who goes the extra mile, who truly cares*

about his students' well-being, and is not just a figurehead. The students under your care are truly lucky to have such a caring, hardworking principal.

We were so grateful and proud when [their son] graduated on Friday, February 11, 2000. We will always remember you for your willingness to help. I have also spoken to other parents of students in your school, and they agree that, when their children have a problem, it is always handled in an expedient manner and you never look the other way.

As you probably already know, your staff is grateful they have a principal they can relate to and communicate with. In the words of George Washington, "The art of leadership is getting something done by someone else because they want to do it."

*Sincerely, ***

xxxxxxx

---

*I chose not to identify the writer of the letter. She did forward a copy to then Chancellor Harold Levy.

The Power in a Name

To answer William Shakespeare's query, "What is in a name? That which we call a rose by any other name would smell as sweet." I would say identity is in a name. Recognition is in a name. Respect is in a name.

There is one "name" story that stands above the rest. I once told a student to hurry to get to class.

She said, "You do not know me. What's my name?"

I said, "Young lady, go to class."

She repeated her last exchange, insisting I did not know her.

I then said, "Brittiney, go to class."

At the top of her lungs, she screamed while she ran to class, "He knows me! He knows me!"

Brittiney smiled every time I saw her after that day. Yes, I continued to say her name.

I earnestly tried to know the names of each of my nearly 2,000 students. It was not easy, but I never stopped trying. I wanted each student to have the respect and dignity of me knowing their name and, to whatever extent, by circumstance as well.

Book III

Student Realities

For too many children, the reality is that adults are not there for them. When I think of how we treat children today, I cannot help but reflect on my first reading of William Golding's *Lord of the Flies*. As in the novel, I think we place our children on an island and tell them to fend for themselves, thus creating their own rules and morals. Our children mimic our behavior. They do as we do, not as we say.

Because of our contradictory behavior, children become confused. In order to protect themselves, children turn to people who look like them and speak their language. This protection may come in the form of weapons, gangs, or complete withdrawal from society. We are quick to tell young people not to join gangs. However, we are slow to provide viable alternatives. We talk to young people about the future, "You need to begin now to prepare for college." There is a problem with this statement. Children live in the present.

"I need to make it home today without getting jumped ... I need to make it through school today without getting caught up in a 'he said, she said' situation."

The following list will illustrate some of the realities that children face in school:

1. Students are more likely to learn from people they trust, like, and respect. They will not listen to adults who are hostile toward them. If a student feels disrespected, he will probably lash out or shut down.

2. Students live day-to-day. They rarely think about long-term consequences for current behaviors.

3. Students think adults talk too much. It is difficult for students to listen to adults unless what is being said is relevant to them.

4. Students are taught how to fail from home and school. Parents say, "I hated math when I was in school." Children interpret this as permission to dislike math. Teachers use failure as a threat. I have heard teachers say to elementary school children, "If you don't behave, you will fail." They meant to say, "If you do not follow my rule, I will fail you." By the time students reach high school, failure becomes an expected and acceptable outcome. How many times have you heard students say, "I *only* failed three"?

5. Students place an enormous amount of importance on the opinions of their peers.

6. Students look to adults for protection. When adults fail to protect them, they follow the laws of nature and try protecting themselves.

7. Students welcome praise. They never tire of positive reinforcement.

8. The so-called tough student has an inner child silently crying to get out. His shell shields his emotional fragility. Have you ever noticed that you have greater success with students when you confront them one-on-one? Outside the view of their peers, they are more likely to drop the shield.

9. Children appear to have a high threshold for fear. Adults often misinterpret this. They say children are not afraid of anything nowadays. They are afraid. They just do a good job at masking their fear.

10. Students have a lot to say. They want to express themselves. While they want to share with adults how they perceive the world, adults are busy trying to interpret the world for them.

I thought you might find these two student stories interesting:

On July 3, 2001, I was at the African Street Festival in Brooklyn, New York. A young man appearing to be in his early twenties approached me.

He said, "Mr. Gassaway. Yeah. You put me out of Beach Channel. Yeah. I got my GED though."

I did not remember this individual. If my math was correct, he was probably nineteen years old when I put him out.

I congratulated him and asked, "Why were you put out?"

He said, "I was running the halls and messing with the honeys [girls]."

This example illustrates a major issue in urban high schools. A sizable group of students is overage for their grade. As principal, I did not want eighteen-, nineteen-, and twenty-year-old students in the same classes with thirteen-, fourteen-, and fifteen-year-old students. This is an urban school phenomenon. Although I knew students had a legal right to attend public school until their twenty-first birthday, they did not have a right to hang out in the halls of Beach Channel. Ironically, child advocates would fight to get nineteen-year-old students with nearly no credits admitted to Beach Channel. I would resist (though often conflicted). Yes, I surmised this individual was probably a victim of his circumstance, but I chose not to sacrifice the education of my younger students. In these cases, I would offer the older students alternative placement in appropriate programs across the city. Principals, across this country, are forced to make similar decisions daily.

I received the following e-mail on June 26, 2003 from a Beach Channel graduate:

> Hi Mr. Gassaway,
>
> You may not remember me, but my sister and I always remember you. After you left BC, I wanted to leave, but I changed my mind in September. Anyway, I graduated yesterday, and I felt wonderful about myself. I graduated with an eighty-five average and a certificate for oceanography without getting pregnant (smile) also. High school is hard, and the younger kids do not know what they are getting themselves into when they cut class, join gangs, have kids, and disrespect elders. I always believe, when a child disrespects their elders, they disrespect themselves. I remember one time at BC when kids did something you didn't like. You got on the PA system and said in a stern voice, "I will find you." Even though I didn't do anything wrong, I felt like you were my dad. You and Mr. Monereau made our school feel safe, like a father would. God watches upon you, and he will bless you.

I have discovered that children value and appreciate respect. Respect plays a major role in their psyche. Notably, many young people expect adults to be rude and disrespectful. That has been their experience. I would go out of my way to be respectful to children. Even when I had to suspend or expel a student, I did it with respect. Respect is the basic ingredient to any healthy relationship.

Principal Realities

The job of an urban high school principal is never done. They face a plethora of challenges on a daily basis. It would be helpful for them to understand what I have coined "principal realities." The following are my top ten principal realities:

1. People will always say you are not doing enough to solve the problem. They are usually part of the problem.
2. If you aim to please, you will never hit your target.
3. There comes a time when you must disregard all of the rules and act in the best interest of children.
4. Leadership may become an intoxicant. If you're not careful, you may become drunk with authority.
5. When you stand up for children, you will become a target. Expect false accusations, usually anonymous.
6. Making decisions will be your dominant activity.
7. The paperwork never ends, regardless of the length of

your workday.

8. If you don't pick up the phone and call the right people, the wrong people will call you.

9. Someone will always tell you that the possible is impossible.

10. Racism is an unavoidable reality. If your children are Black, Latino, or poor, they are more likely to receive an inferior education in your school.

To use a team analogy, a principal is the only player who is required to play all positions on the team. The following are just a few of them:

- Instructional leader
- Visionary
- Community leader
- Problem solver
- Scapegoat
- Parent
- Police
- Cheerleader
- Disciplinarian
- Role model
- Mediator
- Risk-taker
- Decision-maker
- Custodian
- Teacher
- Businessperson
- Student
- Project manager (school construction)
- Psychologist
- Pastor

Gassaway's Principles
for Principals

Actualize: First, see things as they are, not as you would like them to be. Confess the issues, concerns, and problems. Once the blinders are off, you can begin to make meaningful change. Develop a vision. Visions must be shared, collaborative, inclusive, and honest.

Deliberate: Think before you act. Once you go through a decision-making process, make a decision, and let it go. Do not second-guess your decisions. Leadership is making decisions.

Respect: Knowing a student's name is the first sign of respect. Make an effort to know your students by name and circumstances. Model behavior that demonstrates respect for your students. When there is mutual respect, trust is the result.

Empower: Encourage students and staff to lead and participate in school development.

React: Respond to student and staff concerns. A molehill may quickly become a mountain if ignored.

Protect: Always protect children from harmful conditions and practices. These conditions may exist at home or school. Poor teaching or insufficient supplies also constitute harmful conditions.

Listen: Speaking may not be a sign of intelligence. Listen to everyone and everything. Even listen to the unspoken words. Let your actions speak for you. Let the actions of others speak for them.

Communicate: It is a good practice to frequently communicate rules, regulations, and expectations. Students or staff may say, "I was not aware of that rule or policy." Clear communication of expectations promotes and encourages compliance.

Observe: Everyone should talk about the visibility of the principal. Observe classes and school environment throughout the day. What leaders do is limited by what they fail to notice. Your presence should be felt at all times, even when you are out of the building.

Consult: No principal/school is an island. Observe best practices in other environments, and adapt them to your school community. Give everyone a platform to be heard. Even if you disagree, listen actively. Contrary to the myth, principals are not omniscient.

Connect: Get to know your neighbors, including religious institutions, businesses, community boards, police, families, and so forth. Share your vision. Develop a strong community network of support.

Balance: Establish a balance between work and personal life. You risk danger of depression if the lines between work and life are constantly blurred. Plan for work; plan for life.

Book IV

My Wife's Reflections

When I met Bernard Gassaway, he was giving a speech on the Atlanta child murders. This was the early eighties. His passion was evident. I noted, "That's a committed brother." Upon investigation, I found out he had a girlfriend. He wasn't available.

The next time I saw him, a group of us were in his dorm room. We were talking about which club we were going to that night and the details surrounding that. Bernard wasn't concerned about partying. He was doing research. He was so intense, so focused, so single-minded about getting the information he needed for writing his paper. He didn't party with us that weekend.

Our next encounter was the following spring semester. He was no longer involved with anyone. I went to Syracuse to see my good friend Tanya and participate in their Minority Cultural Society's Black History Month celebration. Nikki Giovanni was their guest speaker that weekend. By this time, Bernard was the President of the MCS.

I remember calling my other friend, Ellyn, at her dorm in

Boston and telling her I had decided to not pay any attention to the male half of the population. I was sick and tired of them and their games. I was going to put all my energy into my studies. A couple hours later, Tanya and I went across campus to the cafeteria. I had my new mind-set, and I was focused. Bernard walked by the table where we were sitting. He spoke, hooked his umbrella on the chair opposite mine, and proceeded to the other end of the table to eat his lunch. I thought it was a little strange. But I'd sworn off men by then, so it didn't faze me. Later that evening, after the Black history events of the day, Tanya and I went back to the cafeteria for the MCS party. We were collecting tickets at the door. Bernard walked in. After pleasantries, he asked, "Will you save me a dance?" I agreed. The entire time, I reminded myself of my new anti-man state of mind.

We danced a couple times that night. Then, all of the Black students went to the MCS afterparty at the International House. We partied. Bernard asked me to dance again, a slow jam. I'm beginning to weaken. I start talking to God, "Now God, this is definitely not fair. The very day I swear off men and devote myself to my studies, you send a fine, charismatic, intelligent brother to me. Is this the ultimate test or what?"

That was the beginning of the end. We've been together ever since.

I remember Bernard having two jobs while he was an undergraduate. Both jobs worked with children. He was a lunchroom aide and a group home counselor. By this time, we were dating exclusively, and I would sometimes visit on weekends. The group home job was a night job. The first night of the job, Bernard decided to take a nap so he would be alert that evening. (His usual sleep pattern was to go to sleep around 9:00 PM and wake up around 3:00 or 4:00 AM. He knew he would need a nap to stay awake.) We both nodded out. When he awoke, it was five minutes before the last bus left. This was

Syracuse, New York. Bus service was scarce to none. He flew out the dorm and barely made it.

Part of Bernard's character is not to be late (actually he's early) or absent from any responsibility. That night in Syracuse, I learned that about him, and it still holds true. During Bernard's professional career, he refused to take days off. On most of his jobs, he had perfect attendance. Forget about late! If Bernard is late to something, it's time to worry. On the other hand, I am an artist with an artistic sense of time, so the yin and yang are in full effect in our marriage in this regard.

Recently, we were organizing family photos and something stood out to me. All of the photos of Bernard and I dating included children. Our nieces and nephews at the beach ... the neighborhood kids at the zoo ... young kids surrounding us on a trip to Jamaica. It's a little pitiful to say that our dating (and marriage) revolved around young people. On the weekends, young people were always crashing at our house, or we were packing lunches to take them somewhere. (It was usually some place we always wanted to go when we were children.)

My mother often reminds me of one of her earliest memories of Bernard. He told her how he dreamed of owning a farm and taking care of 100 kids. He's had several "farms" and has taken care of thousands of children since that initial thought.

I actually began working for the New York City Board of Education as a substitute teacher before Bernard. I was a good sub. That means, I was in demand from principals because I had the ability to discipline the classes and actually get them to learn, despite my status as "only a sub." Bernard was still working for the Department of Transportation. We'd exchange our work stories at the end of the day. I apparently made my days sound interesting. When Bernard decided to move to a job where he could make a difference, education looked like a great option. His love for young people, combined with his leadership and organization skills, made this a natural career choice.

I recall a day when Bernard and I were both subbing at PS 40. He was the substitute for the day with a sixth-grade class. I was the relief teacher for his prep period. I could hear the noise as I approached the class. (I kept my maiden name, so the students didn't know we were married. We were Mr. Gassaway and Ms. Lilly.) I felt for the brother when I entered his room. It was bedlam. They were off the chain. I am not a very big person. Most would describe me as petite. Therefore, I never had the advantage of being physically intimidating to students. I had to rely on my other skills. I politely made my way to the front of the room. I located a large dictionary that I raised in the air and brought down with a thunderous crash on a nearby desk while yelling one word, "Quiet!" Bernard later said I even scared him.

I told Bernard he could go enjoy his prep. He left reluctantly. I don't know if he was scared for me or the kids. I had taught this class before. I reminded them of my philosophy. They could behave themselves, as I know they are capable. We would have a great period doing fun, creative things, or they could act crazy. In which case, I'd have to act crazy, too. I never did tell them exactly what my crazy looked like, but they realized I knew how to make learning fun. So, they chose fun. Forty minutes later, Bernard returned to a peaceful classroom. (I also think he gained some respect for the classroom management skills of his tiny wife. He later said he also learned it is important to come prepared with something interesting for the students to do.)

Bernard and I taught in some of the same schools while we were subbing. When Bernard was asked to take a permanent class at PS 40, he accepted. He was pleased to be able to settle down with one class and make a difference. It happened to be that very same sixth-grade class.

This class became Bernard's training ground to become the great educational leader he is today. We worked every evening and weekends to develop motivations for the lessons. Motivation was the key. If he could get them interested in the beginning of the lesson, he had them hooked. As with most elementary school teachers in urban communities, we spent much of our own money on materials and supplies. Bernard spent afternoons and weekends phoning or visiting parents to make them understand that he needed them as partners in their child's education. The surprised look on the faces of some of the parents when they opened their door on a Saturday morning to see their child's teacher was priceless. Not to mention, he was a young, Black man.

Bernard has a way of adopting the young people he meets. These students became our adopted children. It's not uncommon for Bernard to come back from the supermarket today and talk about running into student so-and-so and their children.

After a few years with the board of education, I was fed up with the bureaucracy, politics, and general apathy of the system. I quit. By then, Bernard was on a mission. He was going to make a difference in the lives of students in New York City public schools.

When Bernard asked me to read and edit his manuscript for this book, I knew it would be emotional for me. I didn't realize how painful it would be for me. Bernard has been on a long journey. I have been present for more than half his life.

In reading the several revisions of the book, it occurred to me that Bernard is really being humble in his depiction of the drastic changes he has made in the lives of young people and the tremendous toll—physically and emotionally—it has taken on him.

I've watched him as the system tossed and turned as it does, trying to discourage those who are fighting for the kids. I've seen administrators and staff sabotage Bernard. I've seen him passed over for honors, promotions, and bonuses. I've seen him lied to and lied about. I've seen him risk his life.

There are the stories of taking a gun away from a student in his office, running to break up fights, and being stopped by racist cops (for driving while Black) as he rides through Howard Beach and Broad Channel on his way to Beach Channel. This has happened repeatedly. Education is not supposed to be high risk.

For Bernard, being the principal at Beach Channel was like giving birth to 2,000 students. He felt personally responsible for each of them daily. In some cases, he cared more for them than their parents.

Bernard is too modest to tell the real truth about how he transformed that high school. It was a mess when he arrived, and it was a model school when he left. Bernard probably feels a little guilty to tell how he sacrificed so much of himself and his family to achieve that end. He worked day and night for that school and the children. Even when he wasn't there physically, he was there emotionally. The conversations around the house were always filled with Beach Channel stories. Atiya and I would secretly make faces at each other and say in unison, "Another Beach Channel story." During family trips and vacations, his mind was always back at the school. Our Easter breaks were filled with him monitoring the senior trip to Disneyland by phone. I clearly remember the time we took Atiya to the Philadelphia Zoo. We were about to go into the monkey house, and I saw a lightbulb go off over Bernard's head as he read something the zoo had posted. He tells us to go on without him, as he begins copying the information from the sign. It was something he wanted to take back to one of his teachers. I have hundreds of stories where Bernard would get this glazed look on his face. I knew he was in the "Beach Channel" zone.

One of the reasons Bernard and I have been together for more than twenty-five years is our mutual love and respect for children. Believe me; it was with mixed emotions that I dealt with Bernard's almost obsessive-compulsive way he chose to run his school at the expense of our family life. Let's face it, a man who works from 5:00 AM to 8:00, 9:00, or 10:00 PM and goes out to support the school's sports teams and work with a community-based boys club on the weekends simply does not have time to spend with his family, regardless of how bad he wants to. Bernard is a bleeding heart where kids are concerned. He believed his students needed him more than we did. Some were homeless, hungry, abandoned, or abused. If I was a crackhead, he would have had to save Atiya.* The reality was that I was able to handle things in his absence. He didn't have to worry about home or Atiya.

A man getting beat up daily by a racist system is not always in a pleasant mood when he comes home. Not only is it difficult to operate as a family mostly in his absence, he is exhausted and not a happy camper when he is home.

Now, let me back up here a little. Practically from the beginning of our relationship, Bernard told me he was ready to be a father. He has always related well to children. When we finally had Atiya eleven years ago, I could not have anticipated any of my feelings about being a single parent in a double-parent household.

Bernard and I have never been a couple that has had to be physically together to make our relationship work. During the first five years of our relationship, he was going to school in Syracuse or Albany. Absence really does make our hearts grow fonder. Now we have a child, and time is passing quickly. Before we know it, she'll be grown.

During Bernard's second year at Beach Channel, we were fighting our own educational battle for Atiya. By the time she was four years old, she had been in two schools. The first was a fake

*I don't mean any disrespect to crackheads.

Montessori school. (How can you call yourself a Montessori school when only one of your many teachers is trained in the Montessori method?)

In the second school, where her kindergarten teacher couldn't spell kindergarten, the director felt free to tell us that all of her teachers are bad their first year. A couple of years before that, I had mentioned to Bernard that I wished I could homeschool Atiya. When we were at wit's end with finding a good school for her, Bernard said we should speak to Barry Domfort, the music teacher at BC, and his wife Valerie. They were homeschooling their two daughters. I called Valerie, probably the same day. She sounded like the most peaceful, fretless, well-adjusted mom, let alone home-schooling, mom I ever spoke with. She eased my fears. She made it seem doable. She invited us to a homeschool conference on an upcoming weekend. Bernard was working, so I went by myself. It was a breath of fresh air. The other homeschool families were very open and welcoming.

John Taylor Gatto and Katharine Houk were the speakers. I met well-adjusted, seemingly happy, homeschooled children who shared their experiences. I learned the extremes of homeschooling, from re-creating the classroom experience at home to unschooling, and everything in the middle. I was thrilled to take the information back to Bernard. Homeschooling seemed like the best match for our family. Thank goodness, I was able to work my business from home and be the primary teacher.

So there we were. Bernard was killing himself with 2,000 students during the day. He was involved with the boys club and extracurricular activities on the weekends. He was a member of the Queens district attorney's African-American Advisory Council; he mentored aspiring principals and assistant principals. I was killing myself with one student during the day while running a business and household as well as volunteering at the girls club and community workshops.*

The problem with this picture was that Bernard wasn't spending time with the family, most importantly Atiya. So, Muhammad had to go to the mountain. I began taking Atiya to Beach Channel. I would drop her off. She would at least get to be in Bernard's presence while he completed paperwork and made phone calls. She made friends with the staff and students and was quickly an accepted part of the school community. One of Bernard's assistant principals, who had the same undaunted work ethic as Bernard, had a daughter Atiya's age. Many evenings, they would hang out together with their fathers at the school. Another advantage for Atiya was having the opportunity to feel like she belonged to a school even though she was homeschooled.

I'll fast-forward to the present. In closing, I want to say that I have gained an even greater respect for Bernard over the last three months since he left the board of education. This respect comes from his own acknowledgement that he needed to restore balance to his life if he wanted to be alive to raise his daughter and help raise his adopted community family. His physical health and family health were in jeopardy.

Sometimes, the reasons you fall in love with someone are the very things that challenge your relationship.

Bernard and Atiya play basketball at the park. They go to museums and libraries. They watch boring political shows together. They travel, go shopping, and fuss with each other. Atiya is a beautiful, happy eleven-year-old. She likes boys now. So, if the last eighteen years at the board of education didn't give Bernard a heart attack, a preteen daughter might.

*Anyone who knows Atiya will tell you that she is a handful. She's as intense as her father and me combined. She's intelligent, creative, talented, inquisitive, self-motivated, as well as politically and environmentally conscious. She makes you accountable for who you are. On many days, I also felt like I had a large student population.

Book V

Special Education—
Pipeline to Prison

One day, I went to check on a secluded staircase called the E-wing in Beach Channel. Students found this area to be a safe place to hide because adults did not visit it often ... until I arrived. During this trip, I found a student sitting on the stairs. I asked why he wasn't in class. He cursed me out. This caught me off guard.

I asked, "What's your problem?"

He responded, "I'm special ed!"

This young man was a victim of what I call "special ed culture." He was conditioned to believe his classification gave him permission to cross the line of what would be considered normal, acceptable behavior. Educators ascribe certain behavioral characteristics to children who they classify as learning disabled or emotionally disturbed. Over the years, they have changed the names of the classifications. In the end, they all mean the same thing.

I once saw a particular student acting out. In an attempt to be helpful, a teacher said, "Mr. Gassaway, he's special ed." The teacher, like thousands of his colleagues, has developed a set of characteristics for classified students. According to what many educators believe, but will not say publicly, these students are: Crazy; highly sexual; thieves; untrustworthy; guilty of something; depressed; bipolar; dumb; violent; chemically imbalanced; unclean; crack babies; medicated (or need to be medicated); handicapped; emotionally disturbed; learning disabled; not normal; and hopeless.

If you visit almost any medium- to large-sized urban high school, you will undoubtedly find a school within a school. As I traveled from school to school, I noticed special education classes are either located in the basement or some small corner of the building. The classrooms are small. Some even have smaller-sized furniture. In some schools, they lack books and general supplies. Their classroom space is the first to be given up when general education classes need it. In so many ways, educators demonstrate to these students that they do not count. Because of what adults think and how they behave toward classified children, the children begin to behave according to what they interpret as the script.

Inside the mind of a special ed student:

- *Because you place me in a bubble for all to see ...*
- *Because you expect so little of me ...*
- *Because you think I am not normal ...*
- *Because you place me in tight classrooms with little ventilation ...*
- *Because you give me tests I am not prepared to take because you did not prepare me ...*
- *Because other students see me in the smaller classes and on smaller buses, they tease me.*
- *Because of all of these reasons, I have decided to wear my*

label proudly and shout aloud, "I AM SPECIAL ED!"

Children classified as learning disabled or emotionally disturbed generally do not graduate with a general diploma. In fact, in some school systems, including New York City, administrators find ways to remove these students from their dropout statistics, thus showing a slightly higher graduation rate. The message is clear to these students and their families, "You don't count!"

Look at what's happening in New York City public schools. The small schools movement in New York City has received a large amount of press since Mayor Michael Bloomberg assumed control of the New York City public school system. What has not received an equal amount of press is that many of these schools are exempt from having to accept students who have been classified as requiring special education services. Here's a basic question, "If small schools are so good, why aren't they good for some of our more challenged students?" The truth is in their action, not their rhetoric. Classified students are being excluded because some people believe they do not count.

A special education classification is a predictor for future incarceration. The evidence is clear that Black and Latino males are disproportionately in special education and prisons. Any statistical analysis will illustrate the majority of young people who are incarcerated were either classified before entry or were classified during their period of incarceration. Based on my own childhood and professional experiences in New York City, I speak with complete certainty.

Where do we go from here? Saying we need a complete overhaul of this system would be an understatement. I do not doubt some children suffer from mental illness and may require additional counseling services. However, at the very least, we need to ensure the professionals in this area are the very best. Placing an untrained, uncaring teacher and counselor in front of students is a disservice to our children. It tells them that they don't count.

For far too many children, a special education classification is a death sentence. Labels kill. They kill hopes and dreams.

To attempt systemic reform, we must acknowledge that racism plays a powerful role in the perpetuation of children of color being placed on special education plantations.

Ironically, of all the madness occurring at Beach Channel when I arrived, the most effective department was the special education department. It was led by a no-nonsense administrator. She had effectively built a department with mostly caring teachers and support staff. She did not treat her children as if they were sick. She treated them as she wanted her own children treated.

Labels that Kill

Boy, colored, Negro, nigga, nigger, black, Afro-American, African-American, special ed., dropout, juvenile delinquent, criminal, homeless, gifted, teacher, assistant principal, principal, senior superintendent, father, husband, brother, emotionally disturbed, emotionally handicapped, intelligent, author, distinguished, role model, at-risk, ill-legitimate, bastard, crazy, wild, pothead, fool, thief, talented. All are labels that have been used to describe me.

As a former New York City school teacher, assistant principal, principal, district administrator, and senior superintendent for alternative schools and programs, I have struggled with the realization that children in 2005 suffer from the negative impact of labeling in the same way I suffered when I entered the same system as a student some forty years ago. I have boiled it down to the "business" of education.

Why do we refuse to stop the harmful practice of labeling children? In New York City, as it is across this country, if not the world, we establish a set of labels which we ascribe to children. Each label has a set of expectations associated with it. For example, New York State labels its schoolchildren according to outcomes from standardized reading and mathematics tests. Children are either Level 1, 2, 3, or 4.

Educators frequently refer to their students according to their testing levels and have a clear set of expectations associated with these labels. I often hear principals defend their school's overall performance by saying, "Well, you do know that the majority of my students come to me at Level 1" or "I have a majority of Level 1 and 2 students. What do you expect? Miracles?" To be branded Level 1 or 2 is harmful. Children who are considered Level 1 or 2 are performing below standards. Imagine the psychological effect on a child who is reminded every day that he or she is below standard. This expectation is reinforced by adults who continuously place this child with other children who have received similar assessments. It reminds me of a verse in the Bible referring to a man sequestered in a leper colony. "All the days wherein the plague shall be in him he shall be defiled; he is unclean: he shall dwell alone; without the camp shall his habitation be."* This is what children hear: "Keep all of those kids together so they do not spread their ignorance." This practice of intra-school segregation is detrimental to our children. Children are segregated in schools across this land. It has historical roots. I am not referring to racial segregation, which we all know exists. I am speaking of segregation by labels or classifications. Do you remember the old "CRMD" classes? Where were they located? They were placed in the basement of the schools. Technically, CRMD means Children with Retarded Mental Development. However, in my neighborhood it meant "Crazy, Retarded, and Mentally Disturbed." The labels have changed, but the practice continues.

*Leviticus 13:46, Kings James version

Students who have learned the definitions of the new level labels experience a similar sense of deprecation.

I have seen children cry upon hearing that they are "Level 1." It has gotten so bad that children even refer to their friends or fellow classmates according to their labels. "Tony is Level 1. His is in that bad class."

We need to stop this madness. We are clearly hurting our children. What we are doing to our children is tantamount to giving them drugs. Labeling them has the same effect. It dulls the mind and senses. They experience depression, confusion. It weakens their resolve. Their classroom instruction generally lacks stimulus. The flame is then extinguished. Once extinguished, it is damn near impossible to reignite.

There is nothing new about labels. They are stereotypes. Years ago, I attended a workshop on race relations. We were asked to play a word association game. For example, "What comes to mind when you think of the elderly?" People said, "False teeth, gray hair, funny smell, forgetful, and so forth." Next were Italians, Native Americans, Jews, and Blacks. Now, when I listened to the stereotypes of the other groups, I must admit my sin. I laughed at some of the descriptions, until they got to my group. What comes to mind when you think of Black people? The answers were, "Slavery, ghetto, welfare, poor, and nigger." To say that this had a deep impact on me would be an understatement. Now let's fast forward to how we label or think stereotypically about our children.

The following illustrates one way of thinking:

"Teachers who plan to teach dumb children do not spend much time on planning; whereas, teachers who plan to teach smart children make sure that their lessons are correct. The latter teacher does not want to be caught unprepared by his or her students. No one gives a damn about the dumb student. After all, he is dumb anyway. Right?"

I have visited hundreds of schools and programs over my eighteen years on the New York City Board of Education. It is amazing to see the difference when educators have high expectations for children. I strongly believe that children will behave according to the script they are given. I know I did. Once, I was told I was smart. I behaved accordingly. When I was told I was special ed, I also behaved accordingly. When society told me I did not matter, I said, "Fuck it! I am going off!"

The boy who cannot sit still at four or five years of age is described as having some kind of attention deficit disorder. The boy who can sit still at the same age is described as well-adjusted. What's wrong with this picture? A four-year-old boy is not supposed to sit still for any prolonged period of time. When we force children to act in discord with their nature, they become confused. We then label them.

Listen to the cries of our children:

"I am confused. My nature tells me to mimic the behavior of my parents. When I do what my nature tells me to do, you reprimand me. I watch your behavior and behave like you. Yet, you tell me not to behave that way. I am confused. You call me things other than my name: stupid, dumb, special ed, wild, fool, crazy and Level 1. At first, I did not know how to respond. Now I understand. Do not as you do. Do as you say. Act according to the expectations of the names you give me. Right?"

Why do we refuse to stop labeling our children? It does not pay to stop. In fact, the more we label, the greater the funding sources. Schools cannot get funding unless they are attached to labels. Have you noticed the level of rebranding and creation of new labels? Take the "Leave No Child Behind" legislation for example. Here are a few labels associated with this legislation: Schools in Need of

Improvement (SINI), Districts In Need of Improvement (DINI), and Supplemental Educational Services (SES). Look at the amount of money being made by businesses for SES. SES is a ruse; it serves to pay companies to tutor students who were not taught in the first place. There is no evidence of success. In fact, across the country, companies have sprung up to compete for this burgeoning market. Everybody is getting paid except for the children and poor people. Isn't it interesting how the phrase "Leave No Child Behind" is a play on the military mantra practiced on the battlefield, "Leave no soldier behind"? They should tell the truth about this legislation. It should read, "Leave No Business Behind." Here are some additional money-making terms: disadvantaged youth, at-risk students, achievement gap, after-school programs, bilingual education, charter schools, civics education, drug free schools, education reform, English as a second language, faith-based initiatives, GED, urban education, technology, testing, rural education, special education, and parental involvement. Using these terms to label children will continue as long as money can be made from doing it. It is the American way.

Here's what you can do to be a part of the solution. Change your duplicitous ways. Do not talk tough at home or behind closed doors and cower in the light. Do not be a slave to a promise. Do not follow leaders who continue to walk in circles or double talk. You are witnessing crimes against children. If you remain silent, you are in fact a co-conspirator. Confront your fear. Change your behavior—you can control that. You cannot control others.

No more commissions. No more studies. No more panels. Action is required.

Master of Education

"You cannot serve two masters." You cannot serve children and remain silent while they are being hurt under your watch. You cannot serve children when you promise the master you will remain loyal to him no matter what. Eighteen years ago, I pledged to serve children no matter what. So when I was told, as senior superintendent of Alternative Schools and Programs and Adult and Continuing Education for the New York City Department of Education that I served at the pleasure of the school's chancellor and the mayor, at first, I did not get it.

I contend that most superintendents began their careers as teachers. Teachers take a silent oath to pledge allegiance to their students. Somewhere along the hierarchical ladder, one's allegiance begins to shift. Once you leave the schoolhouse, it becomes difficult to exclusively serve students. You are expected to serve the person or persons who determine the fate of your employment. In the case of school superintendents, that's the chancellor and mayor.

Most school superintendents get it. They understand that by accepting their positions, they can no longer pledge allegiance to children. They understand that there is a line they cannot cross. They understand that they must be careful about what they say. They understand that they cannot express an independent thought, especially if it is not in accordance with the party line. They understand that if they disagree with the party line, they must keep it to themselves.

As teachers, we take pride in the fact that once we close our doors, we can exercise a level of assumed autonomy. "I know I'm supposed to use the workshop model. Who will know if I've used 10 or 15 minutes on this section?" Superintendents cannot close the door so easily and assume anything, let alone autonomy. Autonomy implies a level of independence. Have you witnessed any New York City school's superintendent exercise an independent thought that did not jibe with the stated position of the mayor or chancellor? Superintendents would not dare denounce a flawed educational policy that comes from City Hall or Department of Education headquarters publicly. Some are so afraid that they will not even do so privately. They all got the message back on March 15, 2004, when the mayor exercised his right to remove several members of the Panel for Educational Policy who dared to disagree with him on the issue of ending social promotion for third-grade children. Didn't they know that they could not serve two masters? They were told in the preamble of their by-laws that, "All members serve at the pleasure of the official who appointed them." What were they thinking?

The mayor's actions sent a message loud and clear. If you serve at my pleasure, shut your mouth. Have you heard opposition from any city agency? You definitely have not heard any from the New York City Department of Education. I find it sadly amusing each time I watch the New York City Council hearing with Chairwoman of the Education Committee Eva Moskowitz grilling Department of Education employees. You can see the fear on their faces, hoping that they do not say anything remotely outside of the party line. After all, they were well rehearsed. I am sure they ask themselves as Councilwoman Moskowitz is hammering them, "What would my master want me to say?"

After serving one master, children, for 16 years, I was assigned senior superintendent of Alternative Schools and Programs in July 2003. The first year in this position was exciting. I worked directly with an educational giant, Dr. Lester Young, Jr. He somehow managed to do what so many before him had failed or were afraid to do. He chose to serve children instead of the system.

Under the leadership of Lester Young, we began to make some needed reforms within the larger reform. You see, the *Children First* Reforms did not consider the children we served in my superintendency. *Children First* focused primarily on the elementary grades. Middle and high school children, who have been disenfranchised for years, would have to continue the game of educational roulette. If they were lucky enough to get into a "good school," fine. If not, tough luck. These were the thousands of young children who were pushed through the primary grades long before *Children First*. These were the children who had fallen between the cracks. These were the children who were and are victims of policies that enable some well-meaning, misguided educators to push them out of school. They were homeless, pregnant, court involved, overage and under-credited, illiterate, and poor.

It was during my second year as superintendent, following the retirement of Lester Young, that the phrase "serving at the pleasure" hit home. As we got closer to the mayoral election, I felt the reigns tighten. Although never spoken directly to me, it was clear that I was expected to be a good boy. I was expected to advocate the position of the mayor. However, I could not do this. I knew the reality that many children faced did not match Mayor Michael R. Bloomberg and the school's Chancellor Joel I. Klein's rhetoric. Their standard line was, "Things are improving, scores are rising, but we still have a long way to go."

I represented the children who were on the "long way to go" end of the process. I wanted nothing to do with the bogus talk about test score gains. These so-called gains did not change one thing for the children whom I represented. City Hall and Department of Education officials had one goal in mind—get Bloomberg reelected. The chancellor frequently advocated the mayor's reelection when he appeared on television. When I first heard this, I remember saying to myself, "I don't care about this mayor's reelection."

If our educational leaders (superintendents) are silenced, what chance do our principals, teachers, parents, and children have? Since no one is willing to tell the emperor that he is not wearing any clothes, our children continue to suffer. Our children continue to suffer because we fail to come to their defense. Our children continue to suffer because we compromise our principles. Our children continue to suffer because we refuse to listen to them, hear their cries. Our children continue to suffer because few are bold enough to utter a word in defense of them. Our children continue to suffer because our so-called political, religious, educational, and community leaders are so weak and paralyzed by complicity or fear.

Here's my charge to educational leaders. If you are not going to pledge allegiance to children, shut up and continue to do as you are told to do. Do not pretend to be an educator. Do not pretend to be free. Your children will surely follow your lead.

About the Author

Bernard attended New York City public schools. From high school, he attended LeMoyne College, a catholic school in Syracuse, New York. He was elected President of the Minority Cultural Society in his junior year. He went on to graduate from LeMoyne with a Bachelor of Arts degree in English, in 1982. Two years later, he earned his first Master's degree from the State University of New York at Albany, in public administration.

Bernard worked for two years at the New York City Department of Transportation. In 1986, shortly after his mother passed away, he resigned from the department of transportation to pursue what he called, "meaningful work," and began his teaching career at Public School 40Q, in Jamaica, New York. Two years later, he transferred to Boys and Girls High School where he taught English and computer literacy. After several years as a high school teacher, and a brief attempt to start a small computer consulting business, he returned to teach at Intermediate School 59Q, in Springfield

Gardens, New York. While teaching at 59Q, he completed his second Master's degree in Education Administration and Supervision at Baruch College. Shortly after, he became an assistant principal at Junior High School 192Q, in St. Albans, New York. Six months later, he transferred to become the assistant principal of pupil personnel services at Far Rockaway High School, in 1994.

In April 1997, Bernard was assigned and later appointed the first African-American principal at Beach Channel High School. After his first year at Beach Channel, he was the recipient of the New York State Title I Distinguished Educator Award. In 2001, the Queens Borough President's African-American Advisory Council selected him as Queens Educator of the Year. He also received an award for Educator of the Year from Zeta Phi Beta Sorority, Inc., in that same year.

After five years as principal, Bernard resigned to become the Director of New School Initiative for the New York City Board of Education Alternative Schools Superintendency. In July, 2003, he became Senior Superintendent for Alternative Schools and Programs. He was also selected as a Revson Fellow at Columbia University.

In June 2005, after eighteen years with the New City school system, Bernard resigned to "continue to fight the good fight for children." He is currently an author, child advocate, and educational consultant.

Bernard lives with his wife and daughter in New York City.